THE MYTHOLOGY OF
MEXICO AND
CENTRAL AMERICA

JOHN BIERHORST

THE MYTHOLOGY OF MEXICO AND CENTRAL AMERICA

WILLIAM MORROW & COMPANY, INC.

New York

contents

Preface

The present volume completes a three-part series that began with *The Mythology of North America*, followed by *The Mythology of South America*.

The Mythology of Mexico and Central America is different from its companions in that it surveys the myths of just one, more or less unified area, whereas North America fell into eleven mythological regions and South America into seven. For this reason the book treats its material in greater detail; and it incorporates an anthology of basic myths, unlike the other two volumes in the series.

Indirectly the book relates to yet another project, my English-Nahuatl edition of the Codex Chimalpopoca, to be published within a year or two. A rich and very specifically Aztec source of history and myth, the Chimalpopoca nevertheless has points in common with the whole of Middle American lore. I hope that the book in hand will help to demonstrate that this is true and that the study of all, or most, Aztec and Maya writings can benefit by being placed in context with the mythology of other cultures in the region, both ancient and modern.

I owe a special debt of gratitude to the National Endowment for the Humanities for the translation grant that supported my work on the Codex Chimalpopoca.

During the time spent on the mythology series I have benefited from the kindness and expertise of many individuals, all of whom deserve thanks.

I must mention, first, the people who make it possible for a scholar to survive at the confluence of the Bushkill and Moonhaw streams in the southern Catskill Mountains. They are Robert

Simmons, head of the Interlibrary Loan Department of the Mid-Hudson Library System, and his associates Kathleen Anderson, Susan De Lorenzo, and Dolores Tillou—and at this end of the line, my friends on the staff of the Olive Free Library in West Shokan, Rosalie Burgher, Freda John, and Ruth Ann Muller.

At the onset of this project I had the good fortune to receive, as a gift, copies of two helpful works relating to American Indian mythology, *Lightning and Labyrinth: An Introduction to Mythology* and *At the Beginning: American Creation Myths*, both prepared by Marta Weigle and David Johnson (and duplicated by the Department of English, University of New Mexico at Albuquerque). For this I thank Professor Weigle.

Along the way I was assisted at crucial moments by such knowledgeable people as Elizabeth Benson, Frederick Dockstader, David Guss, Bill Holm, Milland Lomakema, Sr., John Anson Warner, and Elsa Ziehm.

Willard Gingerich, Thomas Grigsby, and Alan Sandstrom were among those who generously shared unpublished research.

David Reuther, my editor at William Morrow and Company, believed in these books before they were written and guided them through the press with rare tact and good sense. Compliments also to Elaine Chubb for her intelligent copy editing.

My wife, Jane, and I have a rule against acknowledgments within the family. I will not be breaking it, I hope, if I call attention to the fact that her name appears on the copyright page in this book, as in all my books.

Finally, a word of thanks to my friend Haig Meshejian, whose knowledge about the Indian people of North, South, and Middle America runs deeper than mine. His good conversations, encouragement, and wide-ranging personal library have contributed steadily to my work—and to these three mythology books in particular.

J.B.

West Shokan, N.Y.

Maps

In Mexico and Central America the names of tribes, places, and mythological characters, though largely taken from Indian languages, are written to be pronounced as in Spanish. Vowels, then, have Spanish sounds (*a* = *ah*, *e* = *eh*, *i* = *ee*, *o* = *oh*, *u* = *oo*). The consonant *j* is similar to the English *h*; the combination *qu* has the sound of *k*; and *hu* and *cu*, if followed by a vowel, are the same as English *w* and *kw*.

The sound *sh*, common in English and in some Indian languages, does not normally occur in modern Spanish. When needed, it is represented by the letter *x*, pronounced *sh* or often simply *s*; or, as in some place names, the letter *x* may be pronounced with the sound of *h*. The combination *tl*, used in Aztec words, is always like the *tl* in *atlas*; it is not pronounced "tull" as in *bottle*. Observe these examples:

Coaixtlahuacan (ko-ah-eesh-tla-WAH-kahn)
Cuauhtitlan (kwow-tee-TLAHN)
Huichol (wee-CHOL)
Jicaque (hee-KAH-kay)
Mixtec (MEES-tek)
Oaxaca (wah-HAH-kah)
Quetzalcoatl (kets-al-KO-atl)
Xut (shoot)

Such a system leaves questions unanswered, and it is certainly not sufficient to permit accurate pronunciation—though it may prevent some of the worst mistakes.

A dangerous subject

Although the word "mythology" is familiar to most people, it cannot be defined to everyone's satisfaction. Even the mere existence of mythology can be called into doubt. Wherever myths are deeply cherished, wherever they touch people's lives, they vanish and become something else. Many would say that they vanish completely.

In other words, myths are what others have; we ourselves have "scripture" or "history."

Among the modern Bribri of Costa Rica, whose creation epics are as remote from the beliefs of the English- or Spanish-speaking world as anything could possibly be, an outsider who asks for *leyendas* (myths or legends) will be told that there are none. One must ask for *historias* (histories).

Conversely, early missionaries in Mexico recorded the sacred histories of the Aztecs and called them *fábulas* (fables). These were compared, unfavorably of course, with the "true" history of the world as revealed by the Bible. Even an important myth like The Sun and the Fire was referred to in the missionary-collected text as a *zazanilli*, the Nahuatl word for "fable," giving the impression that the Aztecs themselves thought of their creation stories as mere trifles.

One way to deal with the contradiction is to abolish myth, as some investigators are inclined to do, and speak only of "narratives."

Another approach is to seek out native terminology and attempt to apply it. For example, old manuscripts reveal that when Aztec scribes translated Aesop's Fables for their own use they called them *zazanilli*. But when they recorded native myths, these were *tlamachiliztlatolzazanilli* (wisdom-word fables); and today a native Nahua writer may still refer to legendary lore as "wisdom fables." Thus it would be possible to distinguish between "fables" and "wisdom fables" when speaking of Aztec traditions.

Similarly, Tzotzil storytellers separate "recent" and "ancient" narratives. Tarascans speak of "false" stories and "true" stories; and among the Yucatec some narratives are mere *cuentos* (tales), while others are *ejemplos* (exemplums).

The Sumu of Nicaragua apparently lack names for the two categories, but they have tales that are usually told by day and other narratives, more serious, that are told at night. In the words of a Mazatec informant from Oaxaca, "There are two kinds of stories: those that are told for entertainment and those that tell us how life used to be."

This book will be concerned with the stories that are heard at night, the tales not told for mere entertainment, the ones that are ancient, true, exemplary, filled with words of wisdom. If all these ideas can be compressed into the word "myth," then perhaps it can substitute for the better term that has yet to be invented.

Even so, the subject must be approached with a certain amount of hesitation, keeping in mind the attitude of many practitioners, who use the expression *delicado* when talking of myth or ritual. *Delicado* in ordinary Spanish means "sensitive," but as used by

Spanish-speaking Indian traditionalists it carries the extra meaning "dangerous."

The search for stories

In the 1930s and 1940s, when myth collecting began in earnest in Mexico and Central America, fieldworkers often met with resistance. In the Mixe villages of Oaxaca, people denied that there were traditional stories. Among the Jicaque of Honduras practically nothing of the ancient creation tales could be found, and for the Mazatec it was reported that the old myths had disappeared. Yet important collections from all these cultures would eventually be recorded.

In the case of the Mixe, elders who knew the stories withheld them for fear of ridicule, not wanting to give their community a bad reputation.

In some instances, group pressure operated to protect the myths from exposure. Describing his experience among the Kanjobal of the Guatemalan highlands, the writer Oliver La Farge reported, "Conditions for securing myths were heavily unfavorable. The villagers watch each other closely. Passing by my house, particularly at night, they would listen to sounds coming through the thin walls, and more than once spoke unpleasantly to Matín Palás because of the myths which they suspected he was telling us."

Such reserve may be traced to the sixteenth century, shortly after the Conquest, when the old myths and rituals were forbidden by Spanish missionaries. In those days the open expression of non-Christian belief could be punished by imprisonment or worse.

Nevertheless, Indian scribes who had learned the alphabetic script were able to record a number of traditional histories during the mid-1500s. Outstanding among those native documents are two Aztec manuscripts, known as Legend of the Suns and Annals of Cuauhtitlan, and the famous Quiché book from Guatemala called Popol Vuh.

At the time, however, there could be no question of publishing these writings or even of translating them. As the anonymous author of the Popol Vuh observes, "Eval u vach ilol re, bizol re" (Hiding his face is the reader of it, the meditator of it).

Those missionaries who themselves recorded myths did so in order to analyze—and refute—the native beliefs. In the case of the missionary-anthropologist Bernardino de Sahagún, myths and other texts were collected as raw material for the study of language. Scientific curiosity was certainly a force behind this effort. But the official reason was that the native language of Mexico City, Nahuatl, had to be mastered for the purpose of preaching to the Indians.

By the mid-seventeenth century the intellectual activity that accompanied the discovery of the New World had subsided, and the early collections made by Sahagún and others began to be forgotten. Two hundred years later, when interest revived, scholars focused on the early material, assuming that little of value was left to be gleaned from living Indian informants.

As late as the 1880s, with the search for traditional lore in North America well advanced and off to a start even in South America, the region between the two continents remained virtually untouched. A decade later the Swiss botanist Henri Pittier de Fábrega was collecting myths among the Indians of Costa Rica, and the Norwegian explorer Carl Lumholtz was at work in northwest Mexico. But, significantly, the collections that resulted were from areas beyond the heartland.

No doubt many agreed with the distinguished anthropologist Franz Boas, who reported in 1912 that the folklore of the region once dominated by the Maya and the Aztec had been replaced by Spanish traditions. During the first quarter of the twentieth century some noteworthy myth texts were in fact published, especially by such German linguists as K. T. Preuss and Walter Lehmann, but the effort did not gain momentum until about 1930.

Younger investigators who believed in the enterprise and who had the gift to overcome native reticence included J. E. S. Thompson for the Mopan, Elsie Parsons for the Zapotec, and Walter Miller for the Mixe. As the stories accumulated, a clearer picture of the region's mythology emerged; and in the 1950s Fernando Horcasitas was able to prepare the first comparative study of an Indian myth from the Aztec-Maya area, an analysis of sixty-three variants of the so-called Flood Myth, or Deluge Myth.

Still more myths were being recorded during these years, and by the 1970s Robert Laughlin could publish a Tzotzil collection with comparative notes securely placing the stories within a framework of Mexican and Guatemalan lore. This was a first for the region—yet it was the kind of treatment that had been possible fifty years earlier for folklorists describing Indian materials from the United States and Canada.

In recent years the search for stories has continued undiminished. Through the 1970s and 1980s important gaps have been filled by Elsa Ziehm, working among the Nahua of Durango; James Taggart, among the Nahua of Puebla; Anne Chapman, among the Jicaque; and Carlos Incháustegui and María Ana Portal, among the Mazatec.

Institutions sponsoring folklore research include Harvard University (through its Chiapas Project), the Instituto Nacional de Antropología e Historia in Mexico, and the University of Costa Rica in San José.

Not to be overlooked is the Summer Institute of Linguistics, an affiliate of the California-based Wycliffe Bible Translators. Since the 1940s, SIL linguists have reached into Indian communities throughout Mexico and Guatemala, publishing grammars, dictionaries, and myth texts with a meticulousness worthy of Sahagún. And like Sahagún, four hundred years before them, they are agents of religous conversion, though this time on behalf of Protestantism.

It is the sign of a changed world that the Wycliffe translators must cover themselves with a scientific mission in order to pursue their religious work, whereas in Sahagún's day it was religious work that served as the shield, behind which the clerics pursued their scientific researches.

Comparing the stories

An examination of the texts collected in the twentieth century shows that Indian people in various parts of the region, though they may speak different languages, are united in their knowledge of certain non-Christian myths. The Indianness of Mexico and Central America is further emphasized when the new texts are compared with the old, revealing a continuity over at least four hundred years.

One of the best known of the older myths is the story of the god Quetzalcoatl's discovery of corn, a myth preserved in the manuscript Legend of the Suns. According to this sixteenth-century Aztec account, the god noticed a red ant bringing a kernel of corn from inside a mountain. He changed himself into a black ant and went along to see for himself. Finally, to make corn available for humans, lightning was used to split open the mountain.

No other Aztec versions are recorded. But we can now see that this is one of the principal Indian myths of the region, with variants ranging from central Mexico to as far south as El Salvador. For purposes of identification the story will here be called The Hidden Corn. Evidently it is not a myth belonging only to Quetzalcoatl. In fact, the god's name is not attached to any of the modern versions.

The wealth of variants also makes it clear that the early Maya knew the story of the hidden corn. Fragments of it are preserved in three Maya documents: the Popol Vuh of the Quiché, the Annals of the Cakchiquels, and the Yucatec Book of Chilam Balam of Chumayel. These fragments are obscure, but when compared with the material now available, it is clear that they are versions of the same basic myth.

Another myth well known to students of Aztec lore is the story of Quetzalcoatl's descent to the underworld, in which he outwits the lord of the dead, seizes a few bones, and sprinkles them with blood to make living people. The tale appears to have been an important one, since it is preserved in three sixteenth-century versions. All three of these texts, however, are from the vicinity of Mexico City, and no modern variants have been reported. From the evidence, then, it would seem that the story is only of local significance, not one of the widespread myths of Mexico and Central America.

Both The Hidden Corn and the story of Quetzalcoatl in the underworld are what folklorists would call tale types. In other words, they are standard plots, made up of several or many incidents that recur from variant to variant.

By contrast, there are some myths so variable that they cannot be called "types." Rather, they are built around a single strong idea, or motif, in combination with lesser incidents that change considerably from one version to the next. These include The Man of Crops (food plants are identified with the body of a man or boy), The Emergence of Ancestors (tribal elders come out of the earth), and The Loss of the Ancients (an early race is destroyed or disappears).

A comparison of several versions of The Loss of the Ancients will show the extent to which the story can vary, while remaining essentially the same at its core.

gl. Illustration #2 about here

As explained by Yucatec storytellers, the first people were dwarfs, the ones who built the ancient temples. Construction work had been easy for them, because all they had had to do was whistle and heavy rocks would move into place. But their labors were performed in darkness, and when the sun rose for the first time, these people turned to stone. Their images can be found today in many of the ruins.

According to the Totonac of central Mexico, the world was originally inhabited by tiny people who were hunters and gatherers. When the sun rose, they were changed into trees, animals, grinding stones, and cooking pots. At the end of the world they will resume their former identity and eat the people who now live on earth.

In the Popol Vuh, the sacred book of the Quiché Maya, it can be read that the gods carved an ancient race from wood. When it became clear that these people were mindless, the gods sent monsters to tear them apart.

The ancient people were evil, according to the Bribri, and it was these evil beings who created all the worthless plants and the crops of little yield. In addition, they made the grinding stones found today in old graves. The god Sibú tried without success to drown them in the ocean. (How he finally got rid of them is not told.)

In northwest Mexico the Yaqui speak of an ancient race called the *surem*, a diminutive, gentle folk who could not stand noise or conflict. One day a tree began talking in a strange language. None of the *surem* knew what it was saying except one little girl. She explained that the tree foretold the coming of the whites, who would bring new weapons, railroads, and bloodshed—even drug problems, according to the most up-to-date versions. Dismayed at the prospect of so much violence, the *surem* went underground to live, and they have remained there to this day.

Modern adaptations of the basically pre-Columbian myth often contain references to Christianity. For example, the Tarascans say that the giants that once inhabited the earth were destroyed "when God decided to bless the world." According to the Lenca of Honduras, the ancients were changed into animals during "God's conquest."

The Ixil of Guatemala believe that the ancients were angels who eavesdropped on God. To punish them, he sent a flood, then a rain of fire. Since there were a few who survived by entering caves, God decided to make them messengers of the people to come. Today, though they cannot actually be seen, they flash like lightning or rumble like thunder. In the words of one storyteller, "They are our keepers."

In this book all such variants will be grouped in the broad category The Loss of the Ancients. But in the distribution maps included with Part Two a distinction will be made between myths of this sort, which are loosely based on a single motif, and the more tightly structured tale types, which follow a prescribed story line. It is to be understood that the *tales based on motifs* vary more widely than the *tale types*.

Middle America and Mesoamerica

Indian stories from the region between North and South America are still being collected and analyzed. Yet enough are already available to permit generalizations about the mythology of Mexico and Central America as a whole—the territory known to geographers as Middle America, stretching from the southern border of the United States to the far end of Panama.

For the purpose at hand, however, Middle America is better defined as beginning in the north with the Seri and Tarahumara tribes, about a hundred miles below the United States border. Other tribes of the borderlands—Papago, Pima, Apache, and various Yuman groups—have mythologies that evidently belong to the northern continent, and for this reason they are here excluded.

On the south the line is harder to draw, because myths in the area centering on Costa Rica have obvious connections to South America. However, the most characteristic motif of lower Central America, The Seeds of Humanity, does not seem to occur beyond the Panama Canal, so the cutoff, somewhat arbitrarily, may be made at that point.

Taking all aspects of Indian culture into account, anthropologists speak of a more limited region, called Mesoamerica, that leaves out roughly the northern half of Mexico and extends only partway into Central America—as shown on the accompanying map. This is the Aztec-Maya area, the region of the so-called high cultures. It will be useful to consider it carefully.

As set forth by Paul Kirchhoff, the Mexicanist who introduced the term in 1943, Mesoamerica is defined by a list of some fifty cultural traits, which, for convenience, may be divided into groups and abbreviated as follows.

Horticulture and plant use : harpoon-shaped digging stick, floating gardens, maguey fiber used for clothing and paper making, cultivation of cacao, grinding of corn softened with ashes or lime.

Clothing and personal articles : turbans, lip plugs, mirrors of polished stone, sandals with heels, textiles adorned with rabbit hair.

Architecture : stepped pyramids, stucco floors, ball courts with stone rings (for a game reminiscent of both soccer and basketball).

Record keeping : hieroglyphic writing, numbers, screen-fold books, eighteen-month calendar, "century" of fifty-two years.

Commerce : specialized markets, "department store" markets subdivided according to specialty.

gl. Map #1 about here

Weapons and warfare : clay pellets for blowguns, wooden swords with stone chips set into the edges, cotton-pad armor, military orders (eagle knights and jaguar knights), traveling merchants who act as spies, wars for the purpose of securing sacrificial victims.

Ritual and myth : sacrifice of quail, human sacrifice, paper and rubber as sacrificial offerings, acrobatic flier dance, pantheon of gods or spirits, 13 as a ritual number, ritual period of $20 \times 13 = 260$ days, good and bad omen days, mythic concept of one or more afterworlds and of the difficult journey in reaching them.

The most spectacular of these traits, including the pyramids, the hieroglyphic books, and human sacrifice, were of course suppressed by sixteenth-century conquerors. Anything relating to the "dangerous" myths and rituals had to be hidden or discontinued. Nevertheless, such customs as the mysterious flier dance, the observance of omen days, and the concept of the soul's difficult journey are still widespread in the region.

Indeed, in the realm of myth Kirchhoff's list can now be much expanded. Part Two of this book presents twenty basic stories, of which sun myths and corn myths and the creation tales labeled Why the Earth Eats the Dead and The Loss of the Ancients are especially characteristic.

In Part Three it will be shown how these basic stories, along with other mythic elements, combine to form whole mythologies. For example, variants of The Loss of the Ancients are put together in multiples of two, three, or four, resulting in a history of the world based on repeated destructions and creations. This, too, is characteristic of Mesoamerica.

Throughout, it will be assumed that Mesoamerica is a single mythological region, with northwest Mexico and lower Central America as border areas sharing at least some of the features of the heartland.

Taken as a whole, Middle America differs from both the northern and southern continents, mythologically speaking. Yet there are similarities worth noting. Though developed distinctively in each region, the emergence motif—the idea that the first people climbed out of the earth—occurs widely in the hemisphere. Twin heroes, the figure of the trickster, belief in a world flood, a universe of layered worlds, and a once-upon-a-time world where ordinary reality is suspended, are all predictable features of Indian mythology, whether of North, South, or Middle America.

A North American tale that extends deep into Middle America, yet is virtually nonexistent south of the Panama Canal, is the so-called Orpheus Myth, in which a bereaved husband seeks his wife in the afterworld. In the region under consideration, this tale will be called The Dead Wife.

As for South America, several typical myths reach northward into the Middle American region, notably The Tree and the Flood, which has been reported in Costa Rica, with a remote and much altered variant among the Mopan of Belize. The *chullpa* myth of Peru is curiously similar to the Mesoamerican Loss of the Ancients. And Kurupira, the Amazonian monster with backward feet, is found as far north as Oaxaca.

Naturally, European influences are also important in Mesoamerican myth and religion. Among Indian cultures today, European Catholicism may be dominant and nearly pure, as among the Tarascans, where older beliefs have largely disappeared; or it may barely dent the surface, as with the Huichol, whose native mythology remains intact. Most Indian communities lie between these extremes, practicing what anthropologists call folk Catholicism, implying either a mixture of Christian and Indian belief or a public display of Christianity with *costumbre* (native custom) observed privately.

Tlaloc is not dead

A final distinguishing feature of Mesoamerican mythology is its capacity to expand beyond itself. Its themes and principal figures impress themselves upon the wider, Spanish-speaking culture, exercising an influence on the modern world. In a limited way this is true of the hemisphere as a whole. Transplanted Europeans in North and South America have always embraced a certain amount of Indian lore as part of their regional heritage.

But in Mesoamerica, where names like Quetzalcoatl, Tlaloc (the Aztec rain god), and Chac (the Maya equivalent of Tlaloc) are household words, the myths are more active, more likely to find artistic, literary, and even social applications.

One reason is that the Aztec and Maya gods are understandable to people of European background. The specialized deities—god of rain, god of fire, goddess of love, earth goddess, lord of the dead—are reminiscent both of the Greek gods and of the saints of the Catholic Church. Thus the Indian spirits are vaguely familiar, even to those who may be made uncomfortable by them.

Another consideration is that the republics of Middle America are heavily Indian. Most people are of mixed ancestry, and those who are confident that they have no Indian blood are in a minority. (An exception must be made for Belize, formerly British

Honduras, with its large population of African descent.)

A third factor is the modern history of revolution. In the early years of the twentieth century, Mexico led the way with a far-reaching program of social change that, in the eyes of many, righted the wrongs of the Spanish Conquest. Nicaragua in the 1980s was in the early stages of its own revolution, as governments in Guatemala and El Salvador tried to keep their Indian and *campesino*, or peasant, populations from following suit. In such a climate, Indian myths become powerful symbols.

Envisioning a new nation, people remember their roots and think of the struggle for a better life as a chance to regain what is rightfully theirs. For many, poetry is a means of expressing the combination of anger and hope that enables them to carry on. Nicaragua, one of the most troubled nations in the hemisphere, has been called the land of poets. Guatemala and El Salvador have also bred poets, and so has Honduras.

The poets are not always welcome in their own countries, however. Some must live in exile. Others, less fortunate, have become *desaparecidos* (disappeared ones), meaning that they have been secretly imprisoned or put to death by governments in power.

Typically, the exiled Salvadoran poet Claribel Alegría laments the injustices suffered by "my remembered country . . . my mythic country." Predicting victory for the forces of change, she writes, "the cycle is closing . . . Tlaloc is not dead."

The significance of such a statement is plain enough to the authorities. Everyone knows that Tlaloc is a god that demanded human victims.

Still capable of inspiring fear, the old mythologies continue to be provocative, even dangerous.

PART ONE

THE
STORYTELLERS

1

Central Mexico

Aztecs and their predecessors

The Aztec empire was less than a hundred years old when Spanish conquerors arrived in 1519. But from its strongholds in the Valley of Mexico, a highland basin halfway between the two oceans, the empire already controlled a territory extending to both coasts and south nearly to the present border of Guatemala.

Although Aztecs spoke a single language, Nahuatl, they were not a single people. Rather, they were a group of tribes each with its separate government, among them the Acolhua, whose capital was Texcoco, and the Mexica, who inhabited the city that was—and still is—called Mexico. Together with the Acolhua and a third Valley of Mexico nation, the Tepanecs, the Mexica Aztecs ruled the empire, collecting taxes from other nations and sending out armies to put down rebellions.

Probably because they were the most powerful of the tribes and because the Spaniards used their city as their own capital, we have come to know more about the Mexica, including their mythology, than we do about other Aztec peoples. When we speak of Aztec myth, therefore, we are usually referring to Mexica traditions, though we do have a few reports from other Aztec communities, including Texcoco and the towns that lay just east of the Valley of Mexico in what are now the states of Puebla and

Tlaxcala.

With the help of picture books that guided memory, Aztec lore was passed orally from generation to generation. The painted records were not writing in the modern sense but more like comic strips without words. Of particular interest were the books called "year counts," which preserved the history of the people, year by year, going back to the beginning of the world. It was in these records that one would look to find creation myths and the deeds of gods and legendary heroes.

Unfortunately, we have no eyewitness accounts of Aztec story-telling, or history-reading, sessions. But from sixteenth-century manuscripts it is apparent that at least some narrators used a style of delivery alternating between story and song. Here, translated from the Nahuatl, is a passage from the legend, The Flight of Quetzalcoatl, telling how the hero and his companions were made drunk by Ihuimecatl and other sorcerers, who had come to oust them from their palace:

> When the sorcerers had gotten them completely drunk, they said to Quetzalcoatl, "My child, may it please you to sing, and here is a song for you to recite." Then Ihuimecatl recited it for him:
>
> > *I must leave my house of*
> > *quetzal, of quetzal,*
> > *My house of troupial,*
> > *My house of redshell.*
>
> When Quetzalcoatl had gotten into a happy mood, he said, "Go get my sister, Quetzalpetlatl. Let the two of us be drunk together."

The story continues in this manner, punctuated with short songs that the narrator presumably chanted.

Tales like The Flight of Quetzalcoatl were taught to young people in schools run by priests. Music, painting, speechmaking, the use of the calendar, and the interpretation of dreams were

4

all part of the curriculum, as well as the myth, legend, and history contained in the year counts. According to the Aztecs, this learning had originated not with their own ancestors but with a more ancient people, the Toltecs, who had built a civilization just north of the Valley of Mexico.

The impressive architecture of Tula, capital of the Toltecs, was already in ruins during the great days of the Aztec empire. In fact, Tula in Aztec times had become a place of legend. Its people were thought to have been superhuman—taller, swifter, and wiser than ordinary mortals. Toltec gardens, despite the cool highland climate, were supposed to have been magnificently tropical, with vegetable crops so huge that the plants could be climbed like trees.

gl. Illustration #3 about here

More mysterious yet was the civilization that had centered on the nearby ruin of Teotihuacán, whose days of glory had come even before Tula. For the Aztecs, the pyramids of Teotihuacán (place-of-spirit-becoming) were a true home of gods. In at least one Aztec version of The Sun and the Fire, a story that accounts for the birth of the sun, it is said that the mythic events took place in a "spirit oven" at this imposing site.

Modern archaeologists, surveying the entirety of Middle America, have identified Teotihuacán as one of the so-called Classic cities. Others include Monte Albán in the state of Oaxaca, Tikal in Guatemala, and Copan in Honduras, all of which flourished during the period A.D. 200–900. Later cultures, such as the Toltec and the Aztec, are said to be post-Classic, while the very early Olmec culture of Veracruz State may be called pre-Classic.

Sculpture, pottery designs, and wall paintings from these ancient civilizations often suggest myths known to have been told by the Aztecs or by modern Indian storytellers. Even at the Olmec site of La Venta, dated 800–400 B.C., archaeologists have found representations of such well-known mythic figures as the feathered serpent, the rain spirit in the guise of a child or dwarf, and the Man of Crops with corn growing from a cleft in his head. Evidently the Middle American myths of today have roots at least two thousand years old.

The modern Nahua

Approximately a million speakers of Nahuatl still live in Guerrero, the Distrito Federal, Puebla, Veracruz, and other central Mexican states. These descendants of the Aztecs, called Mexicano or Nahua, form the largest Indian group in Mexico today.

Having retreated from the cities during the colonial period, the Nahua maintain their culture in small towns and villages. Necessarily, the most colorful features of Aztec civilization have disappeared. Yet the Nahua still cultivate the corn, beans, squashes, and chili peppers developed in pre-Columbian times. Many are still expert weavers. And in some villages, especially eastward, slit drums, native flutes, and the flier dance serve as reminders of the rich ceremonial life of their ancestors.

The term "Indian reservation" is not used in Mexico. Yet Indian villages throughout the republic, including those of the Nahua, have lands that are set aside for the entire community. These may be forest lands where villagers enjoy woodcutting privileges, or arable lands where garden plots, called milpas, are assigned to particular families. Special plots for the support of the church are cultivated as a joint enterprise, and this kind of communal labor is another of the customs that survive from the ancient past.

Myths also have survived, notwithstanding four hundred years of Catholicism. In the mountain villages of northern Puebla State, the area of densest Nahua population, such stories as The Sun and the Fire, The Hidden Corn, and The Flood Myth can still be heard in very fluent versions. In these communities, men are the principal storytellers, and often the tales are exchanged while the men are away from home on seasonal work parties.

6

It is important to realize that the myths are not mere relics of the past but are subtly adapted to reflect current attitudes. In a study made in the 1970s, it was shown that myth versions collected in two Puebla villages differed largely because one of the communities had greater self-government and more contacts with the outside world.

In the more isolated community, where the storytellers were conservative and withdrawn, female characters were presented in an unfavorable light, whereas in the more worldly community the myths were told in such a way that characters of both sexes entered into the story on equal terms.

Contact with the larger world is even more pronounced in the towns of Milpa Alta and Tepoztlán, located less than fifty miles south of Mexico City. The area is of special interest to non-Indian outsiders because it is easily reached from the capital and because the language spoken there is similar to the Nahuatl of Aztec times. In recent years two storytellers from the vicinity of Milpa Alta have become published authors: Doña Luz Jiménez, who contributed myth texts to the now defunct Nahuatl periodical *Mexihkatl Itonalama* (The Mexicano's Almanac), and Carlos López Avila, whose stories and poems appeared in a Nahuatl-Spanish-French edition brought out in Paris in 1984.

Neighbors of the Nahua

On the whole the Nahua are used to outsiders, since there have always been foreigners in their midst. Among these are the Totonac, to the east, the Tarascans, whose homeland is on the west, and the Otomi tribes of the central highlands, living mostly north and west of Mexico City. Like the Nahua, each of these Indian groups has an illustrious past.

Ancestors of the Totonac are said by some to have built the magnificent city of El Tajín, which flourished in Classic times and undoubtedly controlled a far-flung territory. The Totonac are worthy candidates for this distinction, though in fact it is hard to be certain who the builders of ancient cities actually were. In the case of El Tajín, the architects might well have been Huastecs, the northernmost of the Maya tribes.

Less accomplished than the Totonac, the Otomi people held a small but substantial empire in the thirteenth century, controlled by the Valley of Mexico town called Xaltocan. Xaltocan, like Mexico, was an island city, completely surrounded by water.

When Aztecs rose to power, both the Totonac and the Otomi were conquered and became tribute payers. The Tarascans, on the other hand, were never invaded and were able to keep a sizable empire of their own down to the time of the Spaniards. Dissatisfied with Aztec rule, the Totonac and the Otomi joined ranks with the Spanish conquerors, while the Tarascans, not sorry to see their mighty neighbor defeated, stood idly by.

Today these non-Nahua peoples still preserve elements of their ancient lore, especially in Otomi and Totonac communities in northern Puebla State and among a branch of the Totonac known as the Tepehua, who live in Veracruz, immediately to the north and west of the Totonac proper.

The most spectacular survival of ancient custom is the Totonac flier dance, still being performed by costumed acrobats (held by ropes), who leap from a tiny platform atop a one-hundred-foot-high pole erected at El Tajín.

Noteworthy also are the books of magical and religious lore now being produced by the Otomi of San Pablito, Puebla. Some of these handmade items are bound at the edge in the modern manner. Others are folded accordion-style like the pre-Columbian screen-folds. This is a revived art; but the paper itself, of fig or mulberry bark, long used to make cut-out figures of native gods, evidently represents a continuing tradition from ancient times.

In the Western Sierra Madre

"These were the ones who lived far away. In the woods and grasslands, in the wilderness, among the crags is where they lived."

So reads, in part, a description of the mysterious Teochichimecs of the north country, communicated by an Aztec informant in the sixteenth century. Although we cannot identify these Teochichimecs, they might well have been the ancestors of the tribes now living in the rugged district where the states of Jalisco, Nayarit, and Durango come together, four hundred miles northwest of Mexico City.

To the Mexican bureau of Indian affairs (Instituto Nacional Indigenista) this remote area is known as the HUICOT, an acronym based on the names of its three principal tribes, the *Hui*chol, the *Co*ra, and the Southern *Te*pehuan, who share the district with two smaller communities, the Tepecano of Azqueltán, Jalisco, and the Nahua of San Pedro Jícora, Durango. All five groups speak Uto-Aztecan languages, that is, languages related to the Nahuatl of the Aztecs.

For the most part, people of the HUICOT live not in compact villages but in isolated farmsteads called *rancherías*. They do not have a history that includes pyramids, human sacrifice, markets, or empire building. Nevertheless, basic elements of their mythology correspond closely to those of the Aztec-Maya area. Here in the Western Sierra Madre mountains are the northern outposts of such Mesoamerican myths as The Man of Crops, The Flood Myth, and The Sun and the Fire.

Among the Huichol, these and other folkloric elements are embedded in a complex mythology that would appear to be the most elaborate of any Indian group in Middle America today. The Huichol *mara'akame*, or shaman, is the guardian of these mythic traditions, and it is he, or rarely she, who recites them in the all-night sessions designed to communicate with the gods.

The myth performances have been described as chants, with the audience repeating each stanza after the shaman, or with the shaman intoning the stanza, to which a pair of assistants add a refrain.

When giving a myth to an ethnologist, the informant re-creates it in a spoken narrative. Therefore the published myths are not chant texts but straightforward prose texts that are no doubt easier for the outsider to understand. The Huichol story given as myth xii, in Part Two of this book, is such a re-creation.

But even when re-creating the myths as prose narratives, the informant may be in "danger," fearing not only the gods but also his fellow tribesmen. After a session with an ethnologist, one storyteller commented, "Who knows? Maybe someone will work sorcery against me for having told you these 'delicate' things."

2

Oaxaca

Mixtecans

According to records kept by the Aztecs, it was in a year 5 Rabbit (A.D. 1458) that the ruler Montezuma decided to conquer the Mixtecs. The attack was launched against the important market town of Coaixtlahuacan in the northwest part of what is now the state of Oaxaca.

The king of Coaixtlahuacan had been enriching himself with taxes from towns as far away as the Pacific coast. During the inevitable siege, he was killed by Aztec troops, whereupon the Mexica ruler sent for the king's wife, now widow, and appointed her tribute collector for the entire Mixtec country. "Then for the first time," reads the Aztec account, "gold, quetzal plumes, rubber, cacao, and other wealth began coming in; then the Mexica began to feel cheered, thanks to the tribute goods."

Other native records mention bowls of gold dust and strings of jades. It is also known that the Mixtecs excelled in the art of painting books and that these, too, eventually found their way to the Mexica capital.

One of the books, the so-called Codex Vienna, depicts the deeds of a Mixtec hero who strongly resembles Quetzalcoatl. It is part of a small collection of Mixtec codices that have been in Europe since the sixteenth century, and it may even have been obtained by the conqueror Hernán Cortés during the time of his first entry into Mexico City.

Unlike the Aztecs, the Mixtecs after the Conquest did not leave extensive alphabetic-script records of their mythology. Such records could have bridged the gap between the mysterious picture books and the myths that have been collected in modern Mixtec communities.

As the situation stands, the most important Mixtec myth now known, The Childhood of Sun and Moon, seems to have no history prior to the twentieth century. Yet the story, really a cycle of interlocking stories, has all the earmarks of an ancient Mesoamerican tale; and it is told not only by the Mixtecs, but by the two other Mixtecan tribes of western Oaxaca, namely the Trique and the Cuicatec.

These Mixtecan peoples today, like other native Mesoamericans, are mainly farmers who rely on the familiar staples, corn, beans, and squash. At the same time they are able to grow tropical crops such as cacao, a trait which, as in the old days, lends their culture an exotic flavor when compared with that of the Nahua who inhabit the cooler highlands to the north.

Zapotecans

Moving eastward from the Mixtecan area, we continue to find variants of The Childhood of Sun and Moon. Absent elsewhere, the tale is prevalent through much of Oaxaca and is the principal reason for considering Oaxaca State a separate province, mythologically speaking.

The story is frequently told in the villages of the Zapotecan tribe known as the Chatino, where it may be heard along with other tales when people congregate for births, deaths, marriages, and feasts. The versions are remarkably similar from village to village, even down to the finest details. This is because Chatino lore has been standardized by the conditions of migrant labor.

In the fall, when home gardens can be left untended, people begin to seek work on the large plantations, or fincas, where coffee is harvested in the winter months. There is nothing unusual in this. Indian workers throughout southern Mexico and western Central America migrate seasonally to the fincas. Generally it is the men only who make the trip. But among the Chatino, whole families, including young children, are taken along.

Arriving at the plantation, the Chatino are directed to huge shelters, where each family chooses a space and sets up housekeeping. In the communal atmosphere of the shelters, new friends are made and acquaintances from past seasons are renewed. During evening, hours people gather for conversation and storytelling. Small audiences collect around the best narrators, and once again the myths are re-created.

Weeks later, when people have returned to their widely separated communities, they find that their knowledge of Chatino mythology has been improved. In retelling the old stories at local gatherings, they are less likely to forget the twists and turns of the plot, less likely to invent new details to take the place of memory lapses.

Such cohesiveness is not found among the Zapotec proper. In fact those who are called Zapotecs are not a single tribe, like the Zapotecan Chatino, but a family of nations speaking six or more different languages, interrelated to about the same degree as Italian, Spanish, and Portuguese. As a result, the people do not usually think of themselves as Zapotecs but as residents of a particular town or zone.

Zapotecs today are the largest Indian group in Oaxaca, counted as approximately 425,000 persons in the 1980 census. They inherit an illustrious past, having built the Classic civilization that centered on the city of Monte Albán.

Pre-Classic inscriptions at Monte Albán and at sites nearby, suggest that remote ancestors of the Zapotecs were the inventors of the pictographic writing later adapted by the Maya, the Mixtecs, and the Aztecs. It may be added that Zapotecs produced the near-legendary president Benito Juárez (1806–72), the principal political reformer of the nineteenth century and the only full-blooded Indian to have governed Mexico since pre-Conquest times.

Mixe, Zoque, and Popoluca

A people known as the Mixe live in the steep mountain country of western Oaxaca. By language they are related to two other groups, the Popoluca of Veracruz and the Zoque, who live mostly in the state of Chiapas. All three tribes are believed to have a distant kinship with the Maya.

But the Mixe and the Popoluca, and to a lesser extent the Zoque, have a simpler culture than either the Maya, who live to the east, or the Zapotecans immediately to the west and south. Their territory does not include imposing archaeological remains, and comparatively little is known of their history.

Basically, the people are farmers, though they have not abandoned hunting and fishing. In the twentieth century the Popoluca continued to use the bow and arrow.

Looked down upon as primitive by their Indian neighbors, the Mixe and Popoluca tend to be reticent. As a result, their mythology has not been freely given. Walter Miller, who lived among the Mixe on and off over a period of fifteen years, found that it was helpful to have his wife and little daughter accompany him on his field trips. That way he was no longer a strange "single man."

George Foster, who worked among the Popoluca, reported that at the sight of a stranger in the village, women would shut themselves in their houses and remain hidden until the person had passed. Foster understood that stories were told by mothers for the benefit of their children. But the myths and tales he actually recorded were given to him by men only.

Among these tribes The Childhood of Sun and Moon reaches the eastern limit of its distribution. The myth is well developed in versions collected from the Mixe, thanks probably to contact with Zapotecs. The single Popoluca variant published by Foster is rudimentary in the extreme, and the story does not seem to have been reported at all from the Zoque.

More significant, here, is the myth of the culture hero known to the Popoluca as Homshuk, to the Mixe as Kondoy, and to the Zoque as Chalucas. A great adventurer, this young hero defeated enemies and helped establish the world as it exists today. In Popoluca country, Homshuk is regarded as the corn spirit, and farmers regularly make prayers to him so that their crops will not fail.

The Mazatec

The state of Oaxaca is one of the most Indian regions in Mexico. Fully half its population speaks an Indian language, and within its borders there are some fifteen major Indian groups. Tribes mentioned above are among the most populous, and they are also among those for whom at least some mythology has been recorded. Others, each speaking a distinct language, include the Amuzgo and the Tequistlatec of the southern coast, the Chinantec of the northwest highlands, and the Mazatec, whose territory lies just west of the Chinantec.

Of these last, by far the best known are the Mazatec, whose population is estimated at 125,000 native speakers, mainly in the hilly, coffee-growing region surrounding the town of Huautla.

The modern fame of the Mazatec may be traced to visits made in the mid-1950s by the scholar and writer R. Gordon Wasson, who had heard that the Mazatec were adept at using hallucinogenic mushrooms for curing disease. Directed to the wise woman María Sabina, Wasson participated in her nocturnal healing sessions, sampled her mushrooms, and recorded her chants.

Published in Spanish and English, information about María Sabina brought a stream of visitors to Mazatec country, most of them curiosity seekers who wanted to dose themselves with the "little ones," or "saint children," as the mushrooms are called. During the 1960s and 1970s, María Sabina became an international celebrity and found, eventually, that her psychic powers had slipped away. She died in 1985 at the age of eighty-seven.

Imagining her funeral, María Sabina had predicted that on the day of her death someone would twist the neck of a rooster and lay it beside her, so that within four days its spirit would rise up and crow, signaling the moment for her own spirit to begin its journey to the dead land. During the wake, her family would place jars of water, squash seeds, greens, and fruit next to her body, so that she would not become thirsty or hungry while she traveled along. Candles would be burned and a palm cross laid in her hands.

She did not mention that myths would be told. In Huautla the old Mazatec custom of storytelling at wakes has lately been replaced by drinking and card playing. But in more remote communities the stories can still be heard.

The occasions for storytelling are frequent enough, because according to Mazatec custom a wake must be held not only at the time of death, but on each anniversary for seven years thereafter. The sense of obligation that enforces the custom can be very strong.

Describing a Mazatec wake that he witnessed in a village near the Veracruz-Oaxaca border, the anthropologist Robert Laughlin reports that the event almost failed to take place. The son of the deceased had decided he could not observe the sixth anniversary of his father's death. Then, at night, the father came to him in a dream and said, "My son, why don't you care for me? Can't you see that I am hungry?"

The next day the wake was held, complete with food for the dead and storytelling. It might be supposed that the wake would be a solemn occasion. But such is not the case, even where card playing has not yet edged out the myths. As the religious leader of the village stood up and began the myth of creation—"Once there was nothing to be seen, once there was only water"—the audience, perched on mounds of firewood, began to snicker. As the story developed, in characteristic style, leavened with wit and irreverence, the listeners responded by rocking with laughter.

3

Southern Mesoamerica

The Maya of Yucatan

Of the nearly three million people who speak Mayan languages, the largest single group belongs to the Yucatan Peninsula, which is divided among the Mexican states of Campeche, Yucatán, and Quintana Roo and the northern parts of Guatemala and Belize. These Yucatec, or Maya of Yucatan, number approximately three quarters of a million. They live in towns and villages and in the state capital of Mérida, the region's principal city.

The Yucatec are deeply conscious of their past. They are proud to live in proximity to such archaeological sites as Uxmal and Chichén Itzá, and a few villages still keep copies of the old manuscripts known as the Books of Chilam Balam, containing fragments of ancient myth, history, and prophecy. If the Chilam Balam can no longer be read and consulted in Mérida, city dwellers can at least keep in touch with Yucatec customs and the Yucatec language by tuning in the daytime television series called *Volvamos a nuestras raices mayas* (Let Us Return to Our Maya Roots).

18

Stories, especially the "secret" stories, or myths, are not heard as often as they used to be. As elsewhere in Mexico, myths may be told at funerals; but as the wakes have become more boisterous, the stories have been drowned out.

Storytelling, in addition to providing entertainment, was also a form of home instruction. In the old days, young people would be kept indoors night after night while the mother or the father recited traditional lore. One woman remembers that when she was a girl, she and her mother would get into their hammocks, and the mother, after saying a prayer, would tell *cuentos* (stories). Such domesticity today would be regarded as old-fashioned in most parts of the world, including the country of the Maya.

The stories, nevertheless, have not died. In recent years the anthropologist Allan Burns, working in western Yucatán State, has been able to record versions of The Loss of the Ancients, The Dead Wife, and other myths, not to mention ordinary folktales. Initially advised that the stories could not be "told," Burns came to understand that he would in fact be able to obtain them. But they would have to be "conversed."

In other words, the teller must have an assistant, who responds at frequent intervals by saying *ahah* (true) or by making a brief comment or even by asking a question. The audience, then, is listening to a kind of dialogue.

Often the story will end on a personal note that breaks the spell of enchantment. On one occasion, after performing a myth about the black dog of the underworld, the teller and his helper ended with the following exchange, unrelated to the story itself:

"Let's hunt."
"My rifle's broken."
"Where are the parts?"
"I burned them."
"Where are the ashes?"
"Eaten by a falcon."
"Where's the falcon?"
"Went to the sky."

"Where in the sky?"
"Fell."
"Then where did it fall?"
"Went in a well."
"Where's the well?"
"Disappeared."
"Where'd it disappear?"
"Into your belly button."
"True."

Notice that in this little formula, or chain riddle, the roles of the storyteller and his assistant are reversed. Here it is the teller who asks the questions and makes the final comment, "True."

Another, similar method used by Yucatec to break the spell of a myth is to step right into the story. For instance, if the myth ends with the hero setting off for home, the teller may add, "Well, when I came along, he was just arriving."

If the story closes with an unresolved problem, the teller can say, "When I passed by, they were still trying to save him," or, "If I had been there, I would have saved him myself." Such storyteller's tricks have been reported from the vicinity of Chichén Itzá in central Yucatán State and also from the Chorti Maya of eastern Guatemala.

In the state of Chiapas

Ancient Maya customs have been best preserved among the tribes called Lacandon, who live in tiny hamlets in the rain forest of northern Chiapas. Much photographed for their classic Maya profiles, their flowing hair, and their ankle-length tunics, these wilderness people have continued to use bark cloth, dugout canoes, platform beds, hand looms, and the bow and arrow.

But if they are admired by explorers and ethnographers, they are feared by their distant Maya relatives to the south, who believe that the forest dwellers live in the underworld or at the edge of the earth.

Disobedient children are warned that they may be kidnapped and eaten by the Lacandon. Sensational tales are told in which it is said, for example, that the Lacandon "try" their prisoners "with saliva"—taste them with a moistened fingertip—and if they aren't ready for eating, they throw them into a pen to fatten them up.

In fact, the gentle Lacandon are the guardians of a centuries-old religious and intellectual tradition that includes an elaborate mythology and a system of worshipping the old gods by burning incense in hollowed-out ceramic idols.

Rivalled only by the Huichol of the western Sierra Madre and the Bribri-Cabécar of southern Costa Rica, the Lacandon have held on to some of the purest Indian myths in Middle America. In traditional Indian style, the stories are often told in an abbreviated form unintelligible to those not already familiar with the lore. These decidedly artistic variants skim over the plot, focusing on just a few choice elements, whereas special teaching versions, complete in every detail, are told for the benefit of young children.

The future of Lacandon traditions, however, is in doubt. Although in recent years the people have increased in numbers, the forests that support their culture are being rapidly settled by Mexican outsiders—mostly Hispanic, or Ladino, but also including Tzeltalan Maya from the central highlands of Chiapas.

The Tzeltalans, with a population now in excess of 200,000, have lately been spilling into the lowlands in search of employment and new places to live. Upland farmers by inheritance, many have become truckers and migrant workers. In their home country they are divided into two geographical and linguistic groups: the Tzeltal and the more numerous, better-known Tzotzil, immediately west of the Tzeltal.

While on work trips, men have opportunities to tell old stories and learn new ones. Back home, the myths and tales may be repeated at funerals or in the privacy of the family circle or as an exchange between host and guest. Men claim to be the more knowledgeable storytellers, but in the course of a performance they are just as likely to attribute the tale to their mothers as to their fathers.

Tzeltalan culture, including mythology, varies noticeably from town to town. In the 1960s two major Tzotzil collections were assembled, one by Robert Laughlin in Zinacantán, the other by Laughlin's fellow Mayanist Gary Gossen in the community of Chamula about five miles up the road. Unable to separate the myths from the tales, Laughlin was impressed by the unity of Zinacantec narrative lore. Gossen, on the other hand, found an elaborate native classification of oral genres, featuring two principal kinds of narrative, "ancient" and "recent."

In Chamula, as discovered by Gossen, narratives are performed largely in paired phrases, or couplets. Thus a Chamula variant of The Loss of the Ancients begins in this manner:

> There is a story of long, long ago.
> My grandmother told it to me.
>
> It was in the time of the ancients.
> The earth darkened for five days.
>
> It happened that the sun was still bright and clear.
> Then, at midday, it got dark.

The "ancient" narrative continues with a description of how the people were lost:

> There were little children.
> From them sprouted wings.
>
> "You will surely die, mother," said one child.
> And so the child went outside at once,
> Whereupon the child changed into a bird.
>
> The children survived in that way.
> The mothers and fathers of the children died.

Observe that the third, fourth, and fifth lines of the passage just quoted form a triplet. Overwhelmingly, however, the couplet structure prevails in Gossen's Chamula myths. In Zinacantán, by contrast, Laughlin finds that narratives follow the pattern of everyday speech, though there may be a stray couplet here and there.

Couplet structure has also been detected in narratives from Lacandon, Cakchiquel, and other Mayan languages. The point has perhaps been overemphasized by some students of Mayan literature, yet it seems fair to say that this kind of balancing of one phrase against another is a general tendency of Mayan verbal art.

In Guatemala

Two of the most characteristic Mayan myths are The Hidden Corn and the story that may be called Sun and His Brothers. The first of these explains how the corn mountain was split open by thunder; the second tells how Sun's evil brothers climb trees and become monkeys. Both stories are well developed among the tribes of the central and western highlands of Guatemala, and it is this region—not only for its myths, but for its ritual lore and social customs—that may be regarded today as the stronghold of Mayan traditions.

On the west, near the Mexican border, and extending somewhat into Chiapas State are the Mam groups, including Mam, Kanjobal, Jacaltec, Motozintlec, Ixil, and others. More toward the center are the Quichean tribes, including Cakchiquel and Tzutujil in addition to the Quiché proper. Beyond the rugged highlands in the gentler hills to the east, reaching into Belize and Honduras, are the Kekchi, the Mopan, and the Chorti. These and the other Guatemalan Maya groups make up a population of approximately four million.

Among the stories still told in this region are at least some that appear to be rooted in the Classic period of a thousand years ago. Vases excavated from ancient tombs show painted figures that may represent Sun's monkey brothers, the adventures of Sun and his own brother, and other story elements that recur in the sixteenth-century Popol Vuh and again in twentieth-century myth collections.

Presumably, myths of the Classic period were recorded in screen-fold books, now disappeared. In one of the old vase paintings we see a scribe in the guise of a rabbit, witnessing a mythological scene while busily writing in an opened book. Another of the paintings shows a monkey-faced character—the storyteller?—evidently reading from an opened book.

gl. Illustration #4 about here

Four of the ancient Maya screen-folds have survived in museum collections. But these contain ritual and calendrical lore, not myths. Thus the manner in which stories were told or read in Classic times remains a matter of conjecture.

Among the Guatemalan Maya of the twentieth century, myths are told in the home, at the coffee plantation by migrant workers, around the campfire by merchants traveling from town to town, and of course in that ever congenial setting for Mesoamerican storytelling, the funeral.

Reports from the Jacaltec and the Chorti indicate a lively, dramatic style of delivery, with mimicry on the part of the teller and frequent interjections and laughter on the part of the audience. Scholarly contributions, recalling the screen-fold tradition of an earlier age, are currently being made by writers like the Jacaltec Victor Montejo, who has prepared written texts of Jacaltec myths, and linguists like the Quiché Adrián Chávez of Quetzaltenango, who has published his own edition of the Popol Vuh.

Any consideration of the Guatemalan Maya in the late twentieth century must be placed in the context of what some have called a civil war, others a campaign of terror, in which entire Indian communities have been massacred and perhaps as many as a million persons driven from their homes. There has been no comparable crisis since the Spanish Conquest.

The immediate cause may be laid to the Nicaraguan revolution of 1979, which prompted the government of Guatemala to begin a seemingly unending series of preemptive strikes against its own Indian and peasant populations. In addition to those Maya who have been displaced within Guatemala, an estimated 150,000 have been exiled in Chiapas. Hundreds of Kanjobal have fled to the United States, while the Ixil, it is said, have been so decimated that they may never recover as a people.

Ordinary fieldwork, not to mention myth collecting, has been interrupted for many anthropologists interested in the Maya. Yet it is possible that native mythologies will survive and that even now the old myths may be helping to energize the conflict—a subject that will be mentioned again in the final chapter of this book.

Non-Maya tribes

Within a few miles of the Guatemala-Honduras border the territory of the Maya comes to an abrupt end. But Mesoamerica, as defined by anthropologists, continues as a narrow strip along the Pacific coast as far south as the Nicoya Peninsula in northwest Costa Rica.

Sixteenth-century reports from a western Nicaraguan culture known as the Nicarao mention large markets, complex political organization, human sacrifice, screen-fold books, and other traits that establish the Mesoamerican character of the region, at least historically. Today these Nicarao, along with other tribes of the Pacific coastlands, have been absorbed into the Spanish-speaking population of modern Central America.

A tribe still distinguishable as an Indian nation, though its language has recently become extinct, is the Lenca of western Honduras. According to a myth still told, a young girl from Guatemala appeared long ago among the Lenca and became the bride of one of the region's principal mountains, who in those days was a great lord. After the two were married, the girl from Guatemala became a kind of culture hero, teaching her husband to plant and harvest the various crops.

But if the Lenca story implies a Maya origin for the civilization of the southern extremity of Mesoamerica, it is also possible to imagine Aztec sources. The Nicarao, for one, spoke Nahuatl, the language of the Aztecs, and presumably when they migrated south into Central America these northern people brought cultural traits with them—including religious lore. In fact. the old reports mention Nicarao gods that are nearly identical to some of the known Aztec deities. A few scraps of the old stories have also been preserved, though they are not sufficient to permit the reconstruction of Nicarao mythology.

The Pipil, a modern tribe of El Salvador, still speak a dialect of Nahuatl, and many Salvadoran place names are easily recognizable as Nahuatl, or Aztec. As for Pipil mythology, it is unmistakably Mesoamerican, some would say Aztec. On close inspection, though, the Pipil stories seem closer to the Maya versions than to those of the Aztec. If that much could be agreed upon, it would support the observation that a tribe's, any tribe's, mythology is more likely to be determined by location — that is, by the myths of its near neighbors—than by its connection to a distant culture that merely shares its language.

4

Northwest Mexico

The borderland problem

The southwestern United States and the Aztec-Maya, or Mesoamerican, area are the two most intensively studied Indian regions in the hemisphere. In between lie vast stretches of northern Mexico that are ethnographically barren.

But this is not for lack of ethnic groups. Dozens of small tribes once inhabited northeast and north central Mexico. Today, however, these peoples are little more than names in old explorers' and missionaries' notebooks.

On the western side the situation is more encouraging. A few groups, notably the Seri, the Tarahumara, the Mayo, and the Yaqui, have survived with their languages intact. Yet even here the cultures have been considerably changed by contact with Spaniards; and other tribes, not included on the accompanying map, have in fact become extinct.

It is possible, then, to speak of the mythology of northwest Mexico, but generalizations must remain tentative. The most that can be said is that the area seems to belong with the rest of Middle

America, based on the presence of a single key myth, The Loss of the Ancients, and the apparent absence of the great myth cycles characteristic of the North American Southwest.

At this point we may pause to consider briefly the peninsula known as Baja California, geographically part of northwest Mexico, though quite isolated from the mainland.

Beginning in the north, at the California-Mexico border, are a group of Yuman tribes called Diegueño, whose two principal myth cycles, The Dying God and Flute Lure, unquestionably belong to the North American Southwest. A little farther down the peninsula are the remnants of two additional Yuman groups, the Kiliwa and the Paipai, who tell of a dying deity called Metipa, and of a hero known as God-Child. These myths appear to be variants of the Diegueño material.

Among the Yumans of California and Arizona the principal religious ceremony is the so-called mourning anniversary, or Anniversary of the Dead, legitimized by the myth of the dying god. So it is not surprising to read in the eighteenth-century chronicle of Francisco Clavigero that the now extinct Cochimí, the southernmost of the Baja Yuman groups, used to celebrate an Anniversary of the Dead.

Clavigero is also the source for the mythic lore of the long-extinct tribes at the very end of the peninsula, the Guaicura and the Pericu. But the information on these non-Yuman groups is very fragmentary. The Pericu, it seems, told of a culture hero named Quajaip, whose people joined in a conspiracy and killed him, piercing his head with a wreath of thorns.

On the evidence, one might speculate that the Pericu story is a variant of either The Dying God or the life of Christ — perhaps both. In sum, a weak case could be made for including Baja California with North America. A connection with Middle America would be harder to establish.

The Seri

Among the mainland tribes the most unusual are the small group called Seri, the only surviving Indian tribe of northwest Mexico to speak a non-Uto-Aztecan language, to have never grown crops, and to have held out against Catholicism.

Inhabiting an arid coastal region unsuited to farming, the Seri have long supported themselves by saltwater fishing and the gathering of wild plants and shellfish. In the past half-century, commercial fishing has become an important source of cash. But the Seri economy remains small, since the entire tribe, probably never very large, includes no more than about five hundred people.

In recent years a few Seri have embraced Evangelical Protestantism, while the majority still remain unconverted. Traditional Seri religion and mythology, however, have not been extensively described.

Over the decades the old-time myths that might have come to light have remained uncollected, in part because of the people's reticence, in part because of the difficulty in learning their language. Among the few fragments that have been recorded are a series of simple just-so stories with animal characters, oddly reminiscent of the creation tales of central California:

Origin of the moon's spots. Coyote was trying to catch ducks. As he jumped, the ducks flew away, and Coyote landed on the moon, where he can still be seen.

The first death. Death was caused by Coyote and Dung Beetle. Coyote wanted corpses to eat; Dung Beetle, complaining that people stepped on him, wanted revenge. To answer these desires, Coyote killed his own child, and people began to die.

Origin of fire. Fire is from the fly, who made it by rubbing his hands together, as he still does.

But the Seri also have stories of an ancient race of giants, now extinct; and they tell of a long, arduous trail to the land of the dead, guarded by a fierce dog. Such mythic elements imply at least a partial connection with the mythology of the rest of Middle America.

The Tarahumara

Better known than the Seri are the numerous *rarámuri*—as they call themselves—who farm the narrow valleys and dry, steep mountainsides of western Chihuahua State. Called Tarahumara by outsiders, this important tribe has preserved a solid core of ancient custom, especially among the remote bands known as *gentiles* (pagans).

When Carl Lumholtz visited the Tarahumara in the 1890s, he was able to make a small but significant collection of myths, including variants of The Loss of the Ancients and various animal stories not unlike the little Seri myths described above. At least one of the tales had an unusual provenience. Lumholtz reported: "The Crow, who is very knowing, told this story to the Parrot, who told it to the *gentiles*." (The *gentiles*, it should be mentioned, form only a small minority; most Tarahumara consider themselves Catholics.) But in the 1930s, when anthropological field-work among the Tarahumara was resumed, the myths seemed to have died out. One researcher reported that the mythology had "suffered a decline"; and on another occasion he stated flatly that the Tarahumara completely lack "even the simplest sort of mythology or folktales." Perhaps the social gatherings of this people, so he theorized, were "not conducive to storytelling."

Forty years later, however, more persistent (or luckier) field-workers were again finding the old myths. In the community of Cerocahui, it was reported, the people were gathering on winter evenings around a wood stove, drinking the obligatory cups of coffee that no host would fail to offer and no guest would dare refuse. During the course of the evening, stories of "other times" could be heard.

Many of the tales were ghost stories, murder stories, or rumors of supernatural apparitions. Others, somewhat fewer, were myths dealing with the business of creation.

A significant distinction between creation stories and more ordinary tales was obtained by a collector who asked a woman whom he knew to be a churchgoing Catholic whether she had heard a certain myth about the origin of adultery. She replied, "Oh yes! That's a prayer."

Yaqui and Mayo

Even better known than the Tarahumara are the Yaqui of Sonora, State and their closely related neighbors, the Mayo. Their culture is celebrated for the religious drama called Deer Dance, performed not only in Sonora but in the several Yaqui communities that have grown up in southern Arizona. In the Southwest, on both sides of the border, pictures of costumed deer dancers are widely used to promote commerce and tourism.

Yaqui and Mayo speak mutually intelligible dialects of the same Uto-Aztecan language, but the two tribes have quite different histories. Unlike the Mayo, who immediately accepted Spanish authority, the Yaqui over the centuries have earned a reputation for armed rebellion. Not surprisingly, the Yaqui Deer Dance is stronger than its Mayo counterpart; and among the Yaqui, mythology as a whole is in a much better state of preservation.

Modern Yaqui myth collections contain variants of How the Sun Was Named, The Visit to the Animal Master, and The Buzzard Husband, not to mention The Loss of the Ancients, which, taken together, form an obvious bond with the mythology of Middle America.

Myths are told when people gather for the Deer Dance, or they may also be told by men during a work break or in the evening at the fireside. It is doubtful that most or even many Yaqui would know the myths listed immediately above—except for The Loss of the Ancients, which in Yaqui versions is usually referred to as The Talking Tree. This story is known to virtually everyone and has achieved the status of a national legend, much like the *Inkarrí* myth of the Peruvian Quechua or the story of White Buffalo Calf Woman told by the Sioux of South Dakota.

The tale is so named because the ancients, whom the Yaqui call *surem*, were forewarned of their loss by a certain tree that spoke to them, some say sang, in a strange language.

Variants of The Talking Tree are sometimes preserved in written form by the Yaqui themselves, often with literary embellishments. For example, it has been recorded that the tree sounded like "the chords of a harp" or like the buzzing of bees or "like a telephone apparatus." In the Arizona communities, these versions may be written down in Yaqui, Spanish, or English.

Two English-and-Yaqui-speaking authors whose works have been published by the University of Arizona Press are the tribal leader Felipe Molina and the poet Refugio Savala. Savala's *Autobiography* and Molina's *Maso Bwikam* (in collaboration with the literary scholar Larry Evers) both include versions of The Talking Tree.

5

Lower Central America

Southern influences

The Indian peoples of Panama, Costa Rica, and the eastern regions of Nicaragua and Honduras are generally considered to have more in common with South America than with the Aztec-Maya, or Mesoamerican, area.

Traits that might be mentioned would include the use of blowguns, hammocks, canoes, sweet manioc, and bark cloth, also a preference for hunting and fishing rather than agriculture. All these features, however, are found among at least some groups in Guatemala and southern Mexico.

More distinctively South American are the low wooden stools carved with animal faces and the large, multifamily houses, often circular or oval in plan, with high, nearly conical thatched roofs. The stools are still in use, and although the houses, now single-family, are not as large as they once were, the round or oval plan is still occasionally found.

Language provides an even more decisive indicator. Except for the Jicaque of Honduras, all native-speaking Indian groups in lower Central America are related to the Chibchans of the northern Andes.

In the realm of mythology, both southern and northern influences may be detected. In addition to The Tree and the Flood, which is one of the major myths of the southern continent, the presence of such a tale as The Parrot Brides (where the present race of humans originates with a hero and his parrot wife), as well as various motifs including the loathly god (or the god disguised as a poor man), the reverse-footed monster Kurupira, and the origin of soil (at a time when the earth was bare rock), suggests a southern connection.

Mesoamerican—that is, northern—elements include the difficult road to the dead land (with a body of water and a guardian dog) and tales such as The Dead Wife, Why the Earth Eats the Dead, and The Sun and the Fire.

Tribes of the Mískito Coast

In a broad sense the term Mískito Coast refers to the entire Caribbean coastal plain from approximately the Nicaragua–Costa Rica border northward to about a hundred miles within Honduras. Sometimes loosely referred to as "Mískito," "Miskíto," or "Mosquito," the Indian people of this region, in addition to the the Mískito proper, include the closely related Sumu tribe. Both groups, while preserving their Indianness, have intermarried with the former slaves of African descent brought from the Caribbean islands by British pirates in the seventeenth and eighteenth centuries.

Other Indian groups of the region, all speaking Chibchan languages, are the Paya of Honduras and the Rama of Nicaragua, to which may be added the Guatuso, distant relatives of the Rama.

More narrowly defined, the Mískito Coast is a forty-mile-wide strip entirely within what is now Nicaragua. For more than two hundred years this relatively small area, useful as a haven for oceangoing vessels, remained a British protectorate. When Britain finally ceded the Mískito Coast in 1860, there was an agreement that the Indian people would be self-governing—a promise that for Nicaragua has been hard to keep.

Following the Nicaraguan revolution of 1979, the revolutionary, or Sandinista, government clashed with the Mískito, with the result that the Indians formed their own army. Journalists from abroad reported the conflict, and during the 1980s the Mískito became well known to newspaper readers in the United States.

In keeping with the history of their homeland, many Mískito speak English, not Spanish, as their second language. This has made it easy for them to communicate with North Americans, including North American Indians.

In the interest of Indian brotherhood, Iroquois from New York served as official observers at a 1985 peace parley held by the Mískito and the Sandinistas. Later that same year, when the peace talks had turned sour, the Sioux leader Russell Means traveled to Central America and pledged that a hundred North American warriors would come to the aid of the Mískito. In 1987 the Cheyenne poet and warrior Lance Henson published a poetry collection that included a song for the Mískito: ". . . the people suffer in your jungle and our prairies / listen how the wind is a voice in the ears of warriors . . . / we are like you."

Despite the use of English, Chibchan languages in Nicaragua have remained vital. It is true that among the tiny Rama tribe, traditional myths are now passed down in English. But among other groups storytelling continues in the native tongue:

"The narrator starts slowly, as if searching out the story, one word at a time. Gradually, as he identifies with his subject, the pace quickens. Gesturing with his hands, he begins to lose himself, and soon the words are issuing from his lips as though propelled by a force all their own."

So reads a description of informal storytelling among the Sumu in the 1980s. According to an earlier account, Sumu stories were chanted to the accompaniment of drums: "They made a big circle . . . and they positioned a young man and an old man, with the drums in the middle for music. To the rhythm of these drumbeats they would sing the history of their people so that it would not be forgotten; the old men recited it and the young men repeated it."

Today the role of storyteller may be played by a grandmother as well as a grandfather. Stories are told on work breaks during the day, with the more important tales reserved for nighttime sessions.

Though not a region that could be called rich in traditional lore, the Mískito Coast has made a modest contribution to the world's store of mythology, and it is likely that more myths will be preserved in the not too distant future.

The Jicaque

In the year 1866, to escape a campaign of persecution directed against the Jicaque, four women and four men fled into the mountains of central Honduras to begin a new life.

The tribesmen they left behind, in Yoro Department in the northern part of the country, would soon face the confiscation of their lands and the forced disintegration of their ancient customs. Today the Jicaque of Yoro, though numbering several thousand, have all but lost their native language and are nearly indistinguishable from the general population of Honduras.

Jicaque culture has survived, however, among the descendants of the eight "grandparents," who founded the remote settlement now known as Montaña de la Flor, about fifty miles south of the town of Yoro. Becoming the protagonists of a real-life migration legend, the four couples selected the site of their future community and promptly divided themselves into two groups of two couples each.

By the 1970s this unusual population of interrelated families had increased to four hundred souls, still divided into tribal halves, or moieties, each with its own chief. Identified by students of heredity as a genetic "isolate," the community had suffered the burdens that the term implies. Most significantly, 3 1/2 percent of the people were being born deaf.

In addition, Montaña de la Flor had outgrown its environment. Soils were nearing exhaustion and large game had disappeared. Malnourished, the people had become increasingly susceptible to disease. In the words of Anne Chapman, the anthropologist who has been their best friend and observer, the residents of Montaña de la Flor "live under the threat of death."

Simultaneously the people were preserving a complex mythology, which would soon be revealed as one of the most important that has yet been recorded for Middle America. The myths, dictated by the late Alfonso Martínez, were published by Anne Chapman in 1982 under the title *Los hijos de la muerte* (The Children of Death).

As the phrase suggests, the theme of mortality is prominent in this lore. Humans, as opposed to the immortals of ancient times, are called "dead ones," meaning that they are susceptible to attack by the "vapors" that are everywhere in the world. According to one story, the vapors were ushered in with the origin of sexuality. Another tale has it that the vapors arrived when people learned to fight.

Fire, the source of culture, has both immortal and mortal forms. The living fire was used in ancient times to create the various races of creatures. The easily extinguishable fire that we have today is called "fire of the dead."

Understandably, such classic Middle American tales as The Loss of the Ancients, Why the Earth Eats the Dead, and The Dead Wife are not lacking in the Montaña de la Flor collection.

Until 1960 Montaña de la Flor could be reached only by foot or on horseback. At present, with improved communication, the survival of the traditional way of life is in doubt. Whatever the future may hold, the true story of the eight Jicaque grandparents—though they may have been "dead ones" in the mythological sense—will endure as proof that a nation and its culture can hang by a thread and yet regenerate.

The Talamancan tribes

In southern Costa Rica, as the continent narrows to a width of less than eighty miles, the landmass rises sharply to form the Cordillera de Talamanca, the highest mountain range between the Guatemala highlands and the Andes of Colombia. Chirripó Grande, the tallest of the peaks, stands at 12,533 feet.

The river valleys that begin in the Talamanca range are home to two intimately related Chibchan tribes, the Bribri and the Cabécar; a third group, the Boruca, also of Costa Rica; and a fourth, the Guaymí, who live across the border in western Panama.

Native traditions are preserved among all four of these Chibchan peoples, perhaps best among the Bribri-Cabécar, least among the Boruca. Since 1960 a steady flow of publications about, and by, the Bribri have brought to light a mythology of great purity and intricacy, worthy of reaching an international audience.

As in the old days, shamans continue to serve as guardians of the ancient traditions, and storytelling sessions have not lost their ritualistic aspects.

According to one observer, Bribri myths are sometimes sung, a custom that, formerly at least, was reported for the Panamanian Guaymí as well. Available texts reveal narratives in prose, with occasional passages recited in song. Often the chanted material is unintelligible, or "secret" (as in the italicized passage of myth iii, in Part Two of this book).

As elsewhere in the Americas, a principal reason for telling the myths is to instruct the young. This is true even among the Boruca, where an impromptu storytelling might begin with a casual exchange between a grandmother and her grandchildren:

Grandmother: Don't go swimming today because there has been too much rain, and the stream demon could get you.
Children: Who's the stream demon?

38

Thus the grandmother's cue to tell her own variant of a well-known Boruca story.

The Boruca also have more formal, after-dinner storytelling, which takes place in the kitchen house, a building separate from the sleeping quarters. As would be expected, the narrator on such occasions is an older person, even though many of the young people are themselves knowledgeable about the old traditions.

The even greater formality of story sessions among the Bribri and Cabécar has been reported by the modern Bribri author Francisco Pereira, whose careful description will conclude this tribe-by-tribe survey of native peoples and their narrative art. It will be noticed that there are echoes here not only of Boruca customs but of customs that have been recorded for the Sumu of Nicaragua, the Chatino of Oaxaca, the Yucatec Maya, and other cultures of Mexico and Central America. Pereira writes:

"We who are Bribri regard the subject matter of our traditional narratives as true happenings. Not everyone knows how to recite these texts properly. In general the narrators are the *awapa* [shamans], but also there are certain old women who discharge this function, as in the case of Doña Apolonia Hernández, resident of Córbita, Talamanca, who in addition to being a narrator is a magnificent interpreter of traditional songs.

"It is worth mentioning that Doña Apolonia, so far as I know, is the only woman who sings today in the Bribri language and is perhaps the last of the generation that so well exemplifies our tradition, now seriously threatened by the cultural influences of the *sikuápa* [strangers].

"The traditional narratives are not told just any time or any place: almost always they are recited at night and inside the house. Comfortably settled in a hammock—the preferred spot for shamans and important persons in general—the narrator takes the lead in telling the tale, seconded by another, who acts as interrogator. This second person, often though not necessarily, is a shaman, too.

"First the interrogator approaches within two or three meters

39

[six to nine feet] of the narrator, which is the closest permitted by our standards of courtesy, and after exchanging a few words with him on any subject that comes to mind, he hints that he would like him to tell a history.

"The narrator thinks for a moment, then answers, usually, that he cannot do it or that he does not have a history in his head at this particular time. But the interrogator insists, and it is not long before the narrator agrees to the request.

"Affecting a stance for the occasion—sometimes haughty — he clears his throat a few times and at last begins. The reason for clearing his throat is to get the attention of the audience, especially the little ones, who, like all children, make much commotion. The others who are present immediately heed the signal and hush the children.

"Later, during the recitation, the women silently prepare one last bowl of chocolate [a gourd lined with banana leaves and filled with unsweetened hot chocolate] for the shaman and his audience. The children, meanwhile, are quick to sprawl on their beds, where they can listen more comfortably, though many end up asleep. Those who pay attention acquire knowledge of our way of thinking and of our way of looking at the world."

PART TWO

THE

BASIC MYTHS

In keeping with the original sources, the translated texts that follow preserve unusual words, repetitions, and other features that may seem strange to readers of English. Words added to clarify or complete the meaning are enclosed in square brackets, [ ]. Special terms like "milpa" and "Ladino," which have passed into English usage, are not explained in the translations but may be found in the Glossary in the back of this book.

1

Beginnings

myth i : THE EMERGENCE OF ANCESTORS (anonymous, Aztec, translated from the Nahuatl in Mengin, "Unos annales históricos de la nación
mexicana")

*Rare today, the belief that the first people emerged from the earth was once
common in central Mexico and in the region now know as Oaxaca. The account
given here is from a manuscript of 1528, written by an anonymous Aztec using
the alphabetic script learned from missionaries.*

From Colhuacan [ancestor place], from Chicomoztoc [seven cave
place], from Quineuhyan [emergence place], from there they all
departed. From there our ancestors departed at the time the
people originated. This was when they came forth from their
home, from the cave called Chicomoztoc.

They departed in a year 1 Reed, departed on a day 1 Alligator.
When they had departed, they wandered thirteen years in the
wilderness.

gl. Illustration #5 about here

Of hides were their cloaks. Of hides were their loincloths. Of maguey were their sandals, their headgear, their bows, their prayer mats. What they ate were snakes, rabbits, deer, prickly pears, prickly-pear fruits, prickly-pear leaf-pads.

And in the year 1 Flint, fourteen years after leaving Chicomoztoc, when they had gotten to Quetzaltepec, then they all went separate ways.

myth ii : THE MAN OF CROPS (told by Alfonso Martínez, Jicaque, translated from the Spanish in Chapman, *Los Hijos de la muerte*)

The man of crops is typically a young man, sometimes a child. Popoluca mythology makes him the tribal hero, who says, "I am the one who is going to give food to all mankind, I am he who sprouts at the knees." In Aztec, Tepecano, and Tarascan versions he is buried, and corn (or tobacco) grows from his grave. In a myth of the Quiché, corn and other crops spill from the body of Christ immediately following the Crucifixion.

There was a little boy who had been lost. Suddenly he reappeared where his father was working: "Papá, I don't want to live anymore."

[The boy] refused to wear his tunic. Completely nude with his testicles showing, that's how he wanted to be. "I want you to kill me, Papá."

"I don't want you treating me like this," [said the father.] "How could I kill somebody? Besides, you're only a child. I can't kill you."

The boy became angry. He was given a new tunic, but again he threw it away: "Listen, Papá, if you kill me, you'll eat yams and chayotes. They'll grow right here. Kill me, and I'll give you tobacco from my body. From my blood I'll give you sweet manioc, malangas, bananas, chayotes. I'll be born again so that crops to eat can grow from my blood, and tobacco from my body."

"I can't kill you. If you want to die, you'll have to kill yourself."

"If I do it myself, I won't come back to life."

"All right. You've said enough."

The boy stood there thinking, wondering if Tomam [the supreme deity] might have deceived him. He went to the other world to find Tomam and returned with him to earth: "Papá, I still want you to kill me."

"What happened to those crops you promised me?" [replied the father.] "Am I clearing this land for nothing?"

"It isn't time to plant yet," [said Tomam.] "It isn't the season."

"When will that be?"

"May at the latest, or the end of April."

"I'll believe you, if you're telling the truth."

"Don't look for your little boy anymore. I'm going to take care of him, don't worry about him."

The boy went back with Tomam. When they arrived in the other world, Tomam gave orders to his family: "Take care of this boy for me. Let him be nude, as he pleases. With this child I will send seeds to the world of mortals. From him they will plant. That is why I took him."

Toward the end of April the boy returned to earth, bringing seeds for regular bananas and [various] little ones, and sweet manioc, malangas, chayotes, onions, tobacco. He brought them to his father, planted them for him, and disappeared again.

[Tomam said to the father,] "Everything is going to come up now. You're going to be very happy with the little boy."

The man went home and told his wife what had happened: "They're here already! Regular bananas and little ones, sweet manioc, yams!"

The wife went out to the milpa to see for herself: "But I'm afraid. We could lose them the way we lost our child."

The father kept walking around the milpa. No animals were causing damage. But the wife was not confident.

[Her husband said,] "We're not losing them. Tomam gave his promise. I still feel confident. I'm going to eat a banana."

They were eating now. They were annoyed [when they remembered that their] little boy [had refused to wear clothes], but they were eating with confidence. All their other children liked wearing clothes, didn't throw them out but took good care

45

of them, because they didn't have very many. They didn't like to be nude.

Tomam was watching out for them: "How is your work going? Are you all right? Are you eating? You can harvest tobacco now. It's time now. It's ripe now."

The man harvested the tobacco. It was dry in one week, and they toasted the leaves. The very next day some buyers arrived, some Ladinos: "Hey! Don't you have any tobacco?"

"The tobacco is not very good. It's spoiled. I sowed it too close together."

"Give us a little. Just to see how it is."

He offered them a few leaves.

[The Ladinos tried it and said,] "This could break you of the habit!" But they stayed [anyway,] and they made purchases: "I'd like to eat chayotes."

The Indian man went to get some, and he sold a quarter-measure.

[One of the Ladinos said,] "If you have garlic, I'll buy some. It's good for worms. I also need onions, to mix with meat."

"I'll give you a few, even though they're still green."

gl. Illustration #6 about here

He sold twenty-five heads of the garlic and the same of onions. The Ladinos were pleased.

After many years, the little boy returned. He was grown now, but still he was nude. He did not like the shirts of this world, the shirts of mortals. These temporary clothes did not appeal to him, because later they would be all gone. When his mother saw him, she thought, "What a bad boy. He won't wear our clothes."

"I won't come back here again," [said the boy.] "You won't have to think about me. They appreciate me in the other world. I'm going now, Papá."

"Goodbye, then."

"I'm not coming back. I don't want to die [after all]."

"Don't get into trouble with Tomam," [said the father.] That's all I have to tell you. If you get into trouble, he'll send you back here." "Perhaps Tomam will throw me out. But if I misbehave, I'll just let him cool his head."

"Tomam is the one who gives the orders."

The boy had only come to tell his parents goodbye. He [went away again and] never returned. Since we are children of death, the father and the mother [grew old and] died.

myth iii : WHY THE EARTH EATS THE DEAD (written by Francisco Pereira, Bribri, translated from the Spanish in Pereira, "Narraciones")

In payment for the produce we consume—or for the "wounds" we inflict in cultivating the soil—we allow the earth to eat our bodies when we die. As told by the ancient Aztecs, the myth went one step further and justified the custom of human sacrifice. Modern Maya tellings, heavily Christianized, make Adam the first man to work the earth (and to die as a result). Versions with a preliminary episode in which a bat steals soil from the newborn earth, as here, are limited to the Bribri and Cabécar tribes.

Before creating the earth, Sibú [the Creator] made rocks.

The king of bats had been watching what Sibú was doing. And it occurred to him to defecate with great frequency on the rocks Sibú had made.

After a few days, Sibú noticed that woods and grasses, little groves of ceiba trees and palms, were springing up on the excrement.

Then Sibú went looking for the [bat] monster and found him at rest, hanging from the clear sky [roof] of [Sibú's world]-house, and he asked him, "O uncle, what are you eating that these wonderful plants spring up from your droppings? Go back and eat more of the same."

Then the monster went back to Nopátkuo [the underworld]. In those days an old woman lived there with her daughter and her granddaughter. She was called Namásia. Her daughter was called Namáitami.

47

And her granddaughter was called Bénu. That's what the earth was called when it was newborn.

In those days the monster would go there to sip the blood of that little baby. He would bite the child's toes, then sip the blood to feed himself.

No one could get into Nopátkuo. But the monster, yes, he was getting in. All the way to the child's bed.

This was happening because Sibú had invited Namáitami [the child's mother] to be here in this world as his chocolate server. So she was not at home, and the child was being cared for by the grandmother.

The monster took advantage of the mother's absence and the old woman's carelessness to go and eat from the little baby.

It was the work of Sibú. Everything that happened was according to his will. Yet he knew the monster would have to be punished for what he was doing to the little baby. And that's why he pretended not to know anything, and that's why he told him to go back and eat more of "the same." Yet he already knew that something bad would happen to him.

While the monster was on his way to the child's cradle, no one noticed his presence. But [the inhabitants of the underworld] became aware of it when the child screamed, and then they all gave the alarm: "*He-e-e-ei!* What is happening to the child? Who is eating her?"

Some of them ran over to the crying child, while others ran to the door. At the door they found a snare, and as soon as they got there, they saw the monster already leaving.

Now, it is said that this snare was made of just two strong thin cords, crossed in the form of an X. A special device made it work so that it could cut like a pair of scissors: *tasss!*

And when they saw the monster trying to escape, they worked the cords. And he was instantly cut in half: *tasss!*

But he did not die. He kept on running, although he had to use his hands.

When he got back to Sibú, he protested: "O Sibú, because of you they nearly killed me. Now tell me how I'm going to be healed. If I'm not healed, I'll die. It's your fault."

Sibú could see that the monster was in great distress. So he said, "O uncle, don't worry. I will heal you."

Then Sibú took a handful of cotton and put in wadding so that his insides would not spill.

After Sibú had finished the treatment, he said to him, "O uncle, it is done. But I want you to keep your head toward the ground. Do as I say or the treatment will not be successful."

And so this history explains why bats like to hang with their heads down.

Now, they say that when Namásia used to take care of her grandchild, she always rocked her to sleep with this song, accompanied by a rattle:

Ke-e-e-eala, ke-e-eala, isoe-e-eiala wando wilsoe esaeiala ke-e keala oae-e-eao. Kirsoeala wando wilsoe etalsae; ekirelsoe esaeiala ke-e-e; aeroblae ke-e-e, ekerelsoesoeia, wando wilsoe esaeia-ala ke-e-eala ke keala-a-ao. Ikerelsoe esoeialae wando wilso esoeaiala-a-ae-e-e, irelsoe soeiala-a; etalsae esaeiala ke-e-eala akil saeiala-a-ao.

They say the old woman recited the song in a sacred language, and that's why we cannot explain it. But the elders say it refers to all the sufferings the earth was to endure in this world.

That's why the old woman sang the song to her granddaughter whenever she rocked her to sleep.

And when the earth came to this world, she suffered greatly at the hands of human beings during her lifetime, and finally they killed her.

That's why the earth hates humans. And that's why Sibú decreed that all human corpses were to be buried inside her.

The ancestors believed that this was not simple burial but that in this manner the earth took vengeance on humanity.

That's why some people say, "We are of earth, and of earth we will be again."

That's how they tell the history of the earth.

myth iv : OPOSSUM STEALS FIRE (told by Pablo Guerrero, Mazatec, translated from the Spanish in Incháustegui, *Relatos del mundo mágico mazateco*)

This Mexican myth almost always explains why the fire bringer has a bald tail. In an unusual Mixe variant, Opossum is replaced by Fox, and the story tells why the tip of the fox's tail is black. In Nahua and Tepehua variants it is said that Opossum brought fire to warm the Christ child when he lay in the manger.

They say there was an old woman who managed to keep the fire when it had scarcely become separated from certain stars or planets. She was fearless and went to get the fire where it had fallen. She kept it a long time.

Then, after a while, people decided that this fire ought to be for everybody and not just for the old woman. So they went to the old woman's house and asked for fire.

But the old woman was ferocious. She would not give it to anyone.

Time passed, and word traveled that this old woman had managed to keep fire but would not share it.

Then Opossum came along and said to the people, "I, Opossum, promise to give you fire, if you promise never to eat me."

Then everyone made fun of the poor creature. But he remained calm and answered them: "Stop making fun of me, because you are only making fun of yourselves. This very evening you will see that my promise has been fulfilled."

When evening came, the opossum went visiting from house to house, saying he was going to get fire from the old woman, so that others might collect as much of it as they could.

When he arrived at the old woman's house, he said to her, "Good evening, Lady Fire. How cold it is! I'd like to stand next to your fire for a moment and warm myself. The cold is killing me."

The old woman really believed the opossum was cold. And she allowed him to come close to the fire. But this was a clever one, and he kept getting closer and closer until he could put himself into the fire. Then he put his tail down, and that's how he was able to catch it.

When his tail had caught fire, he ran as far as he could, sharing the fire.

And that's why opossums today have a bald tail.

2

Destructions and New Beginnings

myth v : THE LOSS OF THE ANCIENTS (anonymous, Tarahumara, translated from the Spanish in Irigoyen Rascón, *Cerocahui*)

Stories of lost races are among the most characteristic myths of Mexico and Central America. Often the ancient people are giants or dwarves, and usually they are too clever, too evil, or too imperfect to exist in the present world. In some cases they are not killed but merely driven underground, and their power can still be felt. Some versions tell of two, three, or even four previous races, each destroyed in a different manner. Flood is the most frequent catastrophe, though many storytellers mention a too hot sun or an onslaught of jaguars. Christian influence may be detected in the Tarahumara version given here.

In ancient times, too, there were Tarahumara who lived here on earth—say some of the old-timers, so it is said—certain people who lived here on earth in former times, but they were very bad. Then God became annoyed.

God saw that these souls had strayed very far from the path. All sorts of things!

Then he sent the sun to travel down lower, to burn these bad

Tarahumara. But when they started to feel hot, the Tarahumara went into caves, everywhere. They buried themselves curled up, down in the caves, so they they wouldn't be burned.

But the sun came down even lower, and the Tarahumara were just lying there so the heat wouldn't get them, but the sun was too hot, much too hot, like fire, and in spite of everything it burned them. It killed the *rarámuri* [another name for the Tarahumara] who were inside the earth.

The dead who are lying in caves today, whose bones can be seen in the caves, these are the ones that the sun killed, so it is said. That's what those old-timers say.

That's what the elders used to know in the old days. I myself don't know where the story came from. Many Tarahumara are still alive who believe these things, because they can't help themselves, even though they don't wish to believe what the Tarahumara said in the old days and what they themselves are still saying.

But some of us Tarahumara no longer believe what the old-timers say.

My own opinion is, well, it probably isn't true. If it were true, God would have killed all the people. That's why I can't believe it, because we Tarahumara are still alive. We have survived, and we are living. That's why I can't believe it.

So this shows what the old-timers say, but I myself do not believe it. On the other hand, there are certain Tarahumara who still believe in everything. So it seems.

And that is the story of ancient times.

myth vi : THE FLOOD MYTH (told by Serapia Ricarda, Mixe, translated from the German-Spanish-Mixe text in Lehmann, "Ergebnisse einer . . . Forschungsreise nach Mexiko und Guatemala")

This modern variant from Oaxaca is almost identical to the story as preserved in a sixteenth-century Aztec manuscript—which might suggest that the tale is of pre-Columbian origin. Yet the biblical account of Noah's Ark, already well known in sixteenth-century Mexico, would seem to be one of the sources, even if much changed and combined with strictly native material. In some variants the survivor of the flood has a dog who cooks for him. When he discovers that the dog is a woman, he marries her and they produce a new race of humans.

The Old One allowed one man to be in the world, and he said [to him], "My son, this is not the time to work at chores. The whole world is going to be destroyed. The land will become water." He [also] said, "Plant the seed of a cedar tree, and in the morning look for a carpenter to make a big canoe with a lid. Get into it with all your family and seal yourself inside."

In one night, quickly, quickly, the cedar grew up. Wind blew, and the leaves of the tree rustled. [From the tree] the carpenter made a big canoe.

Rain came at midnight. In the night the rain filled the earth with water, and with the water the canoe rose to the sky. The earth and the world were destroyed. The land became water.

Then the water subsided, and the world became dry. There were new people. The Old One allowed others, new people, to exist.

The man came out of his canoe, caught fish and ate them, killed them.

The Old One had said, "You must not make fire."

But up above, the Old One was smelling fire. He came down to see who had made the fire, asking, "Where is this fire smell?"

When the Old One arrived, he said, "Who gave you permission to catch fish?

"And you were not to make fire," said the Old One, "yet you are doing it. I told you not to make fire, you fool. Now you will have to serve as an example for the new people." And the Old One hit him over the head.

"Because you did not listen, I am going to change you into a howler monkey."

gl. Illustration #7 about here

Then the Old One made him into a monkey, putting his face on his rump and his rump where his face had been. Before this, the man had known stories. "But you will forget them all," [said the Old One,] "because you were disobedient. And now I am going to change your children into buzzards and make them eat filth forever."

[He said to them,] "Your father will be the howler monkey. And you, you will be buzzards."

myth vii : THE SEEDS OF HUMANITY (anonymous, Guaymí, translated from the Spanish in Serrano y Sanz, *Relaciones históricas y geográficas*)

According to the tribes of lower Central America, the present race of humans grew from seeds planted by a deity. For the Cabécar and the Bribri these were corn kernels; for the Guatuso, tobacco seeds. In this unusual version from the Guaymí, recorded by a missionary in the early 1600s, the seed is expelled from the body of the deity himself.

With regard to the Flood, they affirm that Noncomala, the supreme god, angry with his province of Guaymí, flooded and drowned it. But their god Nubu retained the seed of a man, which he expelled during dreams and which was sown by Noncomala, no longer angry; and from this were born men and women; and from that [portion of the seed which was] rotten, monkeys.

myth viii : THE TREE AND THE FLOOD (anonymous, Cabécar, reprinted from Stone, *The Talamancan Tribes*)

One of the major myths of the Indians of South America, The Tree and the Flood tells of a tree that is felled with great difficulty, causing a world flood in the process. In some variants the "flood" is a stream, and the story explains the origin of the Amazon or of some other river. In the northwestern corner of South America the myth accounts for the origin of the sea—as it does among the Cabécar and Bribri tribes of Costa Rica.

In the beginning, there was only a large rock and no earth. Sibú [the Creator] wanted earth so there could be people. He sent a beautiful woman named Sea to tell Thunder that he wanted to consult with him [about making the world].

Thunder refused to leave, so Sibú continued to send Sea to persuade him. When Sea became pregnant, Thunder decided to go. Sibú lent him his staff for the trip, [sending Sea to bring it to him,] but Thunder would not accept it and said to Sea, "You brought this for me, [now use it yourself for the return trip,] but don't leave it alone. Take care of it."

In the middle of the trip, Sea said to herself, "I don't understand why I can't leave this club alone. I shall try it and see what happens."

[Later,] when she returned [to look for it], the staff had disappeared. She looked everywhere but couldn't find it. While she was searching, a snake bit her and she died.

Sibú arranged her in a burial package, but she began to swell. He put a frog on top to hold the package down, [to keep it from rising into the air.] The frog grew hungry and jumped to catch an insect he saw passing. Sea popped into the air and became a tree. Her beautiful hair was changed into leaves, and in [the leaves] the parrot, the macaw, and all the [other] birds made their nests.

The tree pushed and pushed upward, piercing the sky which was Sibú's house. He became furious and said, "Listen! What a racket that tree makes forcing its way upward. It won't be long before it will break the air."

So Sibú sent two birds, *tijerita* [a flycatcher, *Tyrannidae* family, or the frigate bird, *Fregatidae* family] and *pajarillo de agua* [a grebe, *Colymbidae* family], to grab the top of the tree and to make a large circle in space. When the two ends met, the tree fell and was converted into water. The nests of the parrot and the macaw were changed into turtles. The leaves became crabs.

[In this way the sea was created, and the surf began to pound.] But the Cabécar know that the noise heard on the shore is the noise made by the wind when it blew through the leaves, which were made from the hair of the beautiful woman, the Sea.

56

The Quest
for Corn

myth ix : THE HIDDEN CORN (anonymous, Mopan, adapted from
Thompson, *Ethnology of the Mayas of Southern and Central British Honduras*)

*The discovery of corn by a small creature, usually an ant, and the breaking
open of the corn mountain by lightning are the essential features of this myth
throughout its many variants. The additional episodes involving the secretive
fox and the impatient woodpecker are typical of the modern Maya. Much abbreviated variants of the story are found in old Maya writings such as the Popol
Vuh and the Book of Chilam Balam of Chumayel.*

Now, at that time the people had no corn or other crops. They
and the animals lived on fruits, also roots that they found in the
forest. However, there was corn in the world. It was hidden
under a great rock. No one knew about it except the leaf-cutter
ants.

One day a fox was going along and found some kernels. The
ants had dropped them as they were bringing the corn out from
under the rock. They had found a way to get down through a

small crack to the hidden supply below.

The fox tried the corn and thought it was good. He waited until night when the ants returned, then followed them until they came to the rock. But he could not get under the rock because the hole where the ants entered was too small. Again he ate kernels of corn that the ants dropped on their way.

When he had eaten, he went to the place where the other animals were. He broke wind, and the others asked him what he had been eating that his wind smelled so sweet.

The fox said he had not been eating anything new, but the animals were suspicious and decided to follow him to see what it was.

After a while, the fox went away. The other animals followed him secretly.

He went back to the ants' trail, where more corn had been dropped. He looked around to see if he could see anyone, and when he could see no one, he began to eat the corn.

But all the other animals were hidden in the bush without his knowing it, and as soon as he began to eat, they came out of their hiding places. "Now we know what you've been eating," they said.

They tried the corn and liked it. Then all the animals waited for the ants to come along the trail, so they could ask them to bring more corn.

The ants agreed. But the animals were so many that the ants couldn't bring enough, and finally they refused to bring any more except for their own use.

The other animals didn't know what to do. They went to the red ants and asked for help. But the red ants were too big to get into the hole.

Then they went to the rat and asked him to help. But he could not get into the hole either.

At last they told the people about this new food, and the people asked the *mam* to help. When the people talked to the *mam*, Yaluk [the greatest of the four *mam*] was not there. So the other three *mam* [or thunder lords] decided to break the rock themselves.

Then each of the *mam* threw a thunderbolt. But they could not break the rock. At last they decided they would have to ask Yaluk. They sent a message to him, saying they needed his help.

Yaluk knew everything that had happened, but he refused to go.

A second time they asked him, and again he refused. He said to the messenger, "Tell them I am an old man. I don't have the strength. They are young men. Let them do it."

Then the other three *mam* sent for Yaluk one more time, saying they had tried to break the rock but could not do it. Then at last Yaluk came.

First he sent the woodpecker to tap the rock to see where it sounded the thinnest. The woodpecker tapped all over the rock and showed Yaluk where it was thinnest.

"Well," said Yaluk to the woodpecker, "that is where I am going to aim my thunderbolt. Hide behind that ledge, and you will be safe. If you stick your head out, you might be killed."

Yaluk gathered his strength and threw a thunderbolt where the woodpecker had shown him, and the rock broke open.

Just as the thunderbolt fell, the woodpecker, forgetting what Yaluk had told him, stuck out his head. A piece of rock hit him, and blood came out. Ever since, the woodpecker has had a red crest.

Yaluk fainted from the great effort he had made, and the other three *mam* rushed forward to snatch the corn.

Now, when the thunderbolt had opened the rock, it had burned much of the corn. Before, all the corn had been white. But now some of it had been badly burned and had turned red. Other kernels were covered with smoke, and they had turned yellow. This was the beginning of red and yellow corn.

The three *mam*, paying no attention to Yaluk, took only the white kernels and ran away to plant them. When Yaluk woke up, he could find only the red and the yellow. These he took, and he made a milpa and planted them.

He was angry with the other three *mam* and said, "They have taken all the white corn, but they will have to plant it three times

59

before it comes up."

And that's what happened. The crops of the other three *mam* failed. Again they planted, and the plants did not come up. Then they went and asked Yaluk why their crops were a failure while his were coming up beautifully.

"I don't know," said Yaluk. He was still angry that they had left him no white corn. "Your crops should do better than mine because you took all the good corn and left me what was burned. I soaked my seed in lime for three days. Perhaps that is why it has been coming up well."

He said this as a joke, because he knew their crop would fail even so. The three *mam* went off and soaked the rest of their seed in lime. Then they planted it. A few plants came up, but the crop was poor.

This is how corn came into the world.

myth x : CORN WOMAN'S MARRIAGE (told by Haciano Felipe, Cora, translated from the Cora-German text in Preuss, *Die Nayarit-Expedition*)

Among the Huichol the myth of Corn Woman's unfortunate marriage is told with much weeping, out of sympathy for the poor heroine, who is made to feel ashamed by her mother-in-law. Accused of being lazy, Corn Woman attempts to grind corn, but all that comes forth is her own blood. In the Cora variant, below, she tries to cook tortillas but merely scorches herself. The corn, or the tortilla made from corn, is her own body.

Here's what happened once. A man was out of corn. He had no more.

Then the ants discovered where corn was. They went there in the evening. They went at night, to get the corn. They came to where a woman lived, who had the corn in her possession.

They stole the corn from her, they took it. They carried it off in the night and brought it home.

When the ants arrived with the corn, the man saw them. "Where are they getting corn?" Then he said to the ants, "Where

60

did you get it? Where is it? I'll go get some, too."

They answered him, "There's none nearby. We bring it from far, if you would go there."

"Yes, I would go."

Then they said to him, "Very well. You'll go with us."

When evening came, they set out, and the man went with them. They walked. But at nightfall they stopped, they wanted to rest for the night. So they set up their camp, and their friend lay down and went to sleep.

They themselves stayed awake. When they saw that the man was sleeping, they went over and chewed off his hair. After that, they left. The man stayed behind, and they never spoke to him again. There he was. He slept on.

When they had gone far, the man awoke and they were no longer there. He raised himself and sat up. "Why did they leave? Why didn't they let me know?"

He just sat there. While he was sitting, the dawn came, and when it was morning, he stood up and looked around. "Where did they go?"

Then he trailed them. They had left tracks. As he was walking along, he lost the tracks, and he trailed them no more. On and on he walked. He came to a place where a bluejay was.

When he got there, he asked, "Where's the corn? I was following some people and lost them and couldn't find them again. They went on ahead."

Then it spoke to him: "I don't know where those people you were following get their corn." And then it said, "Keep going, keep on this path, don't leave it. She lives yonder, my mother lives yonder, along this path. Ask my mother if she has what you are looking for. Perhaps she will tell you."

So he kept going, kept walking until he got there, until he reached the place where she lived.

When he arrived, he asked the woman who was living there, "If you have corn, I've come to get some. Give me a little corn. I was following some people, I don't know what happened to them. They left me behind. They went off while I was still asleep.

61

I couldn't catch up with them. Now I'm asking where corn is. Don't you have it? Then give me some. I have no corn, and corn is what I need. Would you have corn? Then share it with me. I have no corn."

gl. Illustration #8 about here

Again and again he asked. Then he sat down. She didn't answer him. After a while she said, "What did you come for?"

"Ah!" [he said.] "I'm going to get some!"

"Wait a moment. I have to think about this."

Then she asked, "Who told you there was corn here?"

"Alas, it was the ants who told me."

"Ah yes," [she said,] "they robbed me but good."

"They told me I should bring wood ashes, that you needed them [and would trade them for corn," he said].

"So that's what they told you. They mocked you but good. Wood ashes are not valued here. We only use them to kill [ants]."

Then she went into her house, while the visitor sat there. In a few moments she reappeared and asked him, "Did you really come to get some?"

"Yes, I've come to get some."

"Do you need it badly."

"Yes,"

"All right. Wait."

Then she went back inside, and he sat there, waiting. In a few moments she came out again, and she said, "Are you asking me for corn?"

"Yes, I need it badly."

"Are you hurting?"

"Yes, I'm hurting. I have no corn."

"Wait a little longer."

And when she had asked him five times, she said, "Very well. Come in." Then she led him into her house. Inside were many females in human form.

Then she asked him, "Which one do you like?" And he answered, "Am I to take her with me?"

"Yes. You've come to get some, and I've asked you do you need it badly. Whichever one it is, you'll take. I'm showing you these, and whichever you like will go home with you."

"So be it. I'll take this one, the one in the blue dress, [the blue corn.]"

Then she said to her daughter, "You must go now. You must go with the one who has come."

She did not wish to do so, but gradually she made up her mind and said, "I will go, since you really want me to, Mother." Then she went outside with the man.

There were many females, many young ones in white and pale red dresses. These women had dresses of all different colors, speckled, white, yellow, blue, red.

Then the mother went outside and stood silently. At last she said to her daughter, "Now you must do what I say. Do what I say and go home with this man who has come to get corn."

Then she spoke to the man, the one who had come: "You must do what I say. Take my daughter. Do her no harm and treat her well. Don't call out to her, don't give her orders. Keep her in the house, leave her there. There she must stay. Protect my daughter and don't let her make tortillas. Your mother can make the tortillas. Your wife must stay inside."

And then she said, "You must set up two or three storage bins. I'm telling you, build them. So do it."

And with that she sent off her daughter. "Go with this man who came to get corn."

Then they went on their way, they followed the path. They followed along, then they took a rest.

While they were resting, she instructed her husband: "Kindle a fire. We'll eat." He made the fire. Then she told him, "Go get water." And he went for water.

Then she laid out tortillas. They were already there when he came back with water. Then she heated them. And he asked her, "Where did you get the tortillas? We didn't bring any with us."

"I didn't put them there, they just appeared. When I saw them,

63

I heated them up. Go ahead and eat."

He came closer and began to eat. When he had eaten, he settled down and took a rest.

Afterward he started off, walking toward home. He came within a short distance of his house, and when he had come that far, he stopped and said to his wife, "You stay here. I'll tell my mother to tidy the house, so the place can be clean when we arrive."

Then he went and told his mother. He said, "I'm about to move in. I went to get corn and didn't get what I went for. On the way, the ants left me stranded and shaved my head, and when dawn came, I had no more hair. I'm not bringing corn, I'm bringing a wife."

She answered him: "What will you do with this wife? You brought her here and you have no corn?"

"Who knows! I'm bringing a woman. She's waiting close by. Her mother told me we should protect her and not make her work. I'm supposed to keep her inside."

And then he said, "Clean up! I'm bringing my wife here."

The mother did it. She tidied up. Then he brought his wife and put her in the house, and that's where she stayed.

And when evening came, there she was. In the night she got up, took wood ashes, and threw them on the floor. She made them into little piles, threw the ashes and made them into piles.

When she had finished, she lay down again. Everyone was asleep, and the daughter-in-law was inside the house. They were all inside the house, and in the middle of the night they heard the corn gently tumbling into the storage bins.

When morning came, plenty of corn was available. The mother-in-law got up and looked, and corn was in the storage bins.

Also, there was a house, a house that had not been there before. When dawn came, there it stood. And in the morning the daughter-in-law was sitting inside it.

When the old woman's son got up, she said to him, "Come! Look in the storage bin and see if there isn't corn."

Much corn was available. She took a potful to cook, then started to make tortillas. She made them. She ate.

But the wife, who remained inside, was given nothing to eat.

So they had corn, and the wife sat in the house. She stayed inside.

Two days went by. Then the mother-in-law was angry: "What are you doing with this wife you brought here? Why don't you tell her to make tortillas?"

He paid no attention to his mother. And his wife remained indoors. There was much corn in the storage bins. There were bags of it in the house.

Three days went by. Then the mother-in-law exploded: "This wife you brought! Why isn't she making tortillas?"

After five days she spoke up. Five days had gone by. "I will make tortillas," [she said,] "so your mother will not be angry. I will make tortillas."

She left the house and went over [to the kitchen]. Then she reached for a clay pot, took corn, and threw it into the pot. She put it [on the fire], cooked it well, and ground it. Then she looked for wood, built up the fire, stirred it up under the earthenware griddle. And then she began to shape a tortilla.

When she laid the tortilla [on the griddle], the heat scorched her. And so as she ground [more corn], she wept, because the fire had burned her. Then she laid another tortilla.

When five had been laid, her hand stuck [to the griddle]. Unable to free it, she let out with a cry. As she screamed, a gust of wind came along, a whirlwind blew up, and swept her away. With that she vanished and was seen no more. She had returned to her home.

It was early in the afternoon, and her husband, who had been away, was just coming back. Already she was cooking the tortillas, weeping. He could see she was stuck [to the griddle]. He came over and tried to pull her away. He only caught hold of a piece of her armband. He had lost his wife.

She returned to her mother. When she arrived all covered with blisters, her mother would not have her. "Go! I gave you away for that reason, [to provide food.] You must stay there." But [the daughter] would not leave. Instead she sat down and began to cry.

Then her husband went looking for her. There was no more corn, it had all gone away. Nothing was left in the storage bins.

He went after his wife. "She's gone to the place where I got her," [he said.] He came traveling to the house where she lived.

He got there. And when he arrived, he asked his mother-in-law, "Didn't my wife come here? I lost her."

"How did you lose her?"

"She cooked tortillas. Her hand stuck to the griddle and she cried. While she was crying, she vanished."

"Did you treat her the way I told you? Didn't you make her work?"

"No. She cooked the tortillas on her own, and that's how her hand got stuck. I didn't tell her to do it."

"Wasn't your mother angry?"

"Of course. She was enraged."

"Your mother didn't want her, didn't love her. My daughter came home all covered with blisters from the fire. So I don't want to see her anymore. Take her away, I'll give her nothing more. I'm going to undress her. Now take her away."

When she had undressed her, then she brought her out. She was naked when he led her away. "Heal her where the fire has burned her!"

They departed, and he led his wife away. She was naked when he brought her home. That's how she arrived, wearing nothing. Naked she arrived. Just a few rags is all she wore.

She sat down and began to do a little work. Then she hunted for clay and made pots. That's what she did.

Also, she thought of maguey fiber, and she went out with a pack basket to where the magueys grew, and she picked them. When she had picked them, she carried them in her basket and came home with them.

Then she took them out and laid them in water, and they decomposed. She went back and split them, then gathered the fibers and twisted them into cord.

She did weaving and made shoulder bags. That's what she did, sold a few of them and bought a few things in exchange. And so she worked.

Time passed, and that's what the corn woman did. They had no more corn. They would have had corn if the old one had not been angry. The old one became irritable, and then there was no more corn in the storage bins. It disappeared. The wife fled, and it vanished.

That's what happened a long time ago.

myth xi : THE GRASSHOPPERS AND THE CORN (anonymous, Pipil, translated from the German-Pipil text in Schultze Jena, *Indiana*)

This grim little myth not only accounts for the origin of grasshoppers, but serves as a warning against greed. The story line and the moral remain much the same from variant to variant.

There was an old woman who had a son, and she cherished him, she loved him. He was her only child. And when he got married, he went away with his wife.

And he put himself to work, planting cornfields. And when he saw that he was getting rich, he started refusing his mother when she came to buy corn.

He said to his wife, "When that old woman comes, give her nothing. If she comes when I'm about to eat, hide it. She'll want some, but don't give her even a little."

Next time the mother came, the wife was just getting ready to put something down for her husband to eat, and he said, "Here comes the old woman."

Then the wife quickly hid what her husband was eating, and she rushed outside, brought in the dogs, and let the dogs bite the old woman. Then the old woman went away.

Then the wife brought out the food her husband had been about to eat, and he started to eat it. When he had finished, he took a little rest.

Then he got up and went to open the door where he kept his corn. When he opened it, he heard a rumbling inside.

As he stood there, trying to see what it was, a swarm of grasshoppers came out on top of him and ate him up. Then they went into the world and multiplied.

Now, as soon as they were born, they could fly. Then they went to the man's house and overtook his wife and all his children. And they ate them up, the mother as well as the children.

Then the other men and women said, "We mustn't bury these people or we, too, will be eaten. It's because they did wrong, and to their own mother. And if we dare [to touch their bodies], the same could happen to us." And when their bones rotted, a mass of worms came out that ate the corn plants just as the grasshoppers had done.

And that's how it came to be that not everything gets eaten. Although they will strip a cornfield bare, other places they will attack in swarms but not eat at all.

Wherever they go to eat, that place belongs to them. Grasshoppers know where the people live who are like that man who gave them their beginning.

4

Sun Myths

myth xii : THE SUN AND THE FIRE (anonymous, Huichol, reprinted from Lumholtz, *Unknown Mexico*)

One of the best-known tales of central Mexico, this myth tells how a man, or child, leaps into a fire and is changed into the sun; then, usually, a second person enters the fire and becomes the moon. Here, however, the moon appears as the future sun's mother. Recalling sixteenth-century Aztec variants, the text below goes on to explain how the sun came to receive sacrificial offerings of corn beer. In Aztec lore, the offerings were human beings.

In the beginning, there was only the light of the moon in the world, and the people were much inconvenienced. The principal men came together to see what could be done to give the world a better light.

They asked the moon to lend them her only son, a weak, one-eyed boy. She first objected, but at last consented.

They gave the boy a full ceremonial dress, with sandals, plumes, and tobacco gourds, and his bow and arrows; and they painted his face. They then threw him into an oven, where he

69

was consumed; but the boy revived, ran under the earth, and five days later arose as the Sun.

When the Sun radiated his light and heat over the world, all the nocturnal animals—the jaguars and the mountain lions, the wolves, the coyotes, the gray foxes, and the snakes—became very angry, and shot arrows at him.

His heat was great, and his glaring rays blinded the nocturnal animals; and with eyes closed they retired into caves, water pools, and trees.

Still, if it had not been for the gray squirrel and the gigantic woodpecker, the sun would not have been able to complete his first journey across the sky. These two were the only ones who defended him; they would rather die than allow the Sun to be shot, and in the west they placed *tesvino* [corn beer] for him [as a sacrificial offering], so that he [would have the strength to] pass [through the sky]. The jaguar and the wolf killed the gray squirrel and the gigantic woodpecker, but to this day the Huichol offer sacrifices to these hero-gods and call the squirrel father.

myth xiii : HOW THE SUN WAS NAMED (told by Ambrosio A. Castro, Yaqui, reprinted from Giddings, *Yaqui Myths and Legends*)

Huichol variants of this little myth make it clear that the newly created sun cannot rise into the sky until it is named. But in a variant from the Nahua of Durango, the creature who names it, crying, "Sun has appeared!," runs away for fear of being punished as a know-it-all. Both ideas are implied, though not stated, in the Yaqui variant given here. Naturally, the event takes place in the myth time, or time of the surem, *who were an ancient race that disappeared into the earth when the present way of life was established.*

At the beginning of the era of the *surem*, nobody knew the name of the sun and they wanted a name for it. For this reason they held a council on the bank of the Surem River. Everyone gave his opinion, but no name was found for the sun. Every day they studied the matter. They did not know if it were man or woman and so they couldn't decide whether it would be best to give it a male or a female name. The *surem* could not agree. They finally invited all the animals of the world to come to a council.

Once they were all present, before the sun came up, at the edge of the river, they made a great group of men and animals. When the sun appeared, a badger came out of a hole where he lived in the ground.

The badger came to the council and said in a strong voice, "The sun, being a man, comes out of a hole in the earth as I do." Speaking thus, he ran away.

Everyone ran after him, wishing to pay him honor for his great intelligence. They wanted to give a fiesta for him and to pay him well with abundant food.

But the badger ran away and went into his hole and would not come out. He thought they wanted to punish him. From that time on, the badger has rarely gone out on the plains. He is still afraid that they might punish him for something.

myth xiv : THE CHILDHOOD OF SUN AND MOON (anonymous, Chatino, translated from the Spanish in Bartolomé, *Narrativa y etnicidad entre los chatinos de Oaxaca*)

Normally brothers, Sun and Moon are brother and sister in Zapotec, Popoluca, and Mixe variants of this typical Oaxaca myth. As told in certain Mixe and Chatino communities, the story opens with an episode in which a young woman is magically impregnated, dies, and is torn open by a buzzard, who delivers the two children the young woman had been carrying. The remainder of the tale follows the plot of the Chatino variant given here. Notice the incident in which Moon's face is imprinted with the image of a rabbit—a widespread motif in central Mexico and Oaxaca.

In the ancient time, Sun and Moon were people, and they walked the earth.

One day while they were walking along on the earth, the Night Terror found them and started to chase them. The Night Terror was their enemy, the one who was against them. It did not want Sun or Moon to exist, because it was jealous of them.

Sun and Moon ran and hid in a river. But this river was an arm of the sea, and the water began to fall. The river began drying up. The little boys were just about to be caught when an old woman came to get water, and they saw her and asked her to save them from the Night Terror.

So the old woman hid them inside her mouth. She put one in each cheek, and her head became round as a ball. As she was walking back to her house, the Night Terror met her and asked her what was wrong that her head was so round.

The old woman said she had a toothache, and that's why her face was all swollen. So the old woman fooled the Night Terror and carried the little brothers home.

When they got to the house, they stayed there, and the old woman took care of them as though they had been her own children.

The little boys were very naughty. They played all day and made mischief. The old woman worked at her spindle, spinning cotton. But she could never finish, because whenever she left the house to go outdoors, the little boys took up the spindle and tangled the thread.

Time passed, and the little boys believed that the old woman was their mother.

When the brothers were bigger, they began to go out and hunt, and in order to hunt they made bows and arrows.

With their bows and arrows they hunted all kind of animals. They hunted doves and brought them home for the old woman to cook.

When the old woman went outdoors, the boys asked her where she was going, and she said she was going to see their father. But the little brothers did not know who their father was. And they were very curious to meet him.

Then one day they asked the old woman, "Mamá, who is our father? We want to see him."

But the old one answered, "I go very far to meet your father, and I do not want you to find him, because you would be able to kill him."

One day when the old woman went to look for her husband, the brothers decided to follow her to find out who their father was. They followed the old woman to spy on her. And they left a trail, a trail of little leaves and ashes so they would not lose their way.

When the old woman got to a certain place in the forest, the children saw her making strange signals and heard her calling to someone. Soon a large deer appeared, and the old woman gave it the food she had brought.

When they saw this, the brothers returned to the house. They got there before the old woman.

The next day the old woman asked them to go out and cut grass for her husband, telling them the husband ate only greens. Then the brothers went outdoors and made a wooden blade to cut the grass.

They cut the grass with such energy that they frightened a rabbit, and it leaped up in Moon's face. It hit him so hard, Moon's face was left with the imprint of the rabbit. And that's why, today, holy Moon has the rabbit's picture on his face.

The next day the brothers decided to spy on their father, and they set off on the track they had laid, following the trail of leaves and ashes. When they got to the place where their mother had called to the deer, they imitated the gestures the old woman had made, and the big deer appeared.

As soon as the twins saw it, they said, "This can't be our father. It's so ugly. See how skinny its legs are. They look like reed stems. It would be best to kill it."

When the deer came closer, Sun shot an arrow and killed it, and when it was dead, they butchered it. They cut open the body and took out the heart, the liver, and the intestines. Then they put all the insides together and grilled them to make the dish called *skualyku*. They made it and ate the whole thing.

gl. Illustration #9 & 10 about here

Except the liver. They saved that to bring to their mother.

Before leaving for home, they took the empty deer hide and filled it with wasps and arranged the hide so that it looked like a deer reclining, just lying there.

Then they went back to the house and gave the liver to the old woman, who was very glad to have a thing so delicious.

The old woman was about to eat, but before she bit into it, the liver cried out, and the woman felt something was wrong. As she was eating, a frog began to sing, and its song said, "You are eating the flesh of your husband." Three times it sang this song.

"Could it be true what the frog says? Did you kill my husband?" asked the old woman.

"No, Mamá. Don't pay attention to the frog, because it just tells tales," said Sun and Moon.

But the old woman was suspicious nevertheless. And she went to look for her husband. Before she left, she gathered greens, the greenest and the freshest, for her husband to eat.

As she was going along, a crab appeared and told her that the deer was dead. But the old woman did not believe it, and she stepped on it so hard, she squashed it. She flattened it. And that's why, today, the crab is flat.

Then the dove gave out with its call, *suliuu* [it's lying down!], and the old woman thanked the dove, because she believed it was her husband who was lying down. But it was only the hide of the deer, held in position with stakes.

When she saw it, she began to be angry. She thought her husband was taking it easy when he should have been working. So she cut a stick and began to beat the deer, scolding it at the same time.

When she struck it, the wasps started out through a hole in the skin. In their fury they stung the old woman, and her whole body was covered with wasp stings.

The old woman ran off screaming with pain. As she ran along, the rabbit said, "Jump in the water, Mother! Jump in the water, Mother!"

But the old woman answered, "That would do me no good. Better to go to my house, where my children can make me a sweatbath."

When she got home, the brothers prepared the bath, gave her plenty of fire, and put on green medicine leaves so the smoke could heal her.

But the bath was so hot, she perspired greatly, perspired so much she began to burn up, and she told them to take her out of the sweathouse.

But the brothers said, "Here you will stay, holy Mother, and you must eat of the food that will be offered by your children, those who will be born in future times. If the children do not feed you, they will die. All will appeal to you for strength."

That's why, when a little boy or a little girl is born, people make a ceremony and bathe the baby in the sweathouse. Copal and candles are offered, and the Holy Grandchild [Christ?] is spoken to, so that He may eat [the smoke]. Chickens, tamales, tortillas are offered so that the old woman will keep sickness from touching the baby. Prayers are offered to the holy fire, because it is like the sun. We do it this way because the old woman, the mamá of Sun and Moon, set the example.

When the old woman became ashes, Sun and Moon went into the woods and fields. But their hearts were sad. They thought how their mother had lived in darkness. They wondered how to shine light on their mother, to keep her out of the dark.

Then they decided to rise to the sky, and one would shine light by day, the other by night, to brighten their mother's life.

They went to the highest mountain, and Sun brought his staff, and Moon brought a skein of his mother's cotton thread. As they walked along, a snake with shining eyes appeared. They wanted its eyes.

They were intent on removing the eyes of the snake. With the thread they strangled it, with the staff they hit it, until the snake was dead and they got its eyes.

Moon grabbed the right eye, the bright one. Sun got the left eye, the one that shines much less.

With their shining eyes they kept on going. And Moon used his thread to bring down a honeycomb out of a tree.

He ate all the honey. It left him thirsty.

Sun drove his staff into the earth, and springs appeared, water flowed out. That's how Sun drank.

Moon was very thirsty and asked for a little water. But Sun said he would give him water only if they traded eyes. Moon agreed, because of his thirst, and that's how Sun got the brighter eye. That's why his light shines more than Moon's.

Then they went to the mountaintop, and Sun threw the skein of thread into the air. He threw it so hard, it reached the sky. Yet the end of the thread remained in the brothers' hands.

Moon wanted to climb up first. But Sun said the one with the brighter eye should climb first to light the way. Moon did not like this arrangement, but he obeyed him, and that's how the two rose into the sky, one in front, the other behind.

And that's how they go around the sky today, shining light on their mother's grave.

myth xv : SUN AND HIS BROTHERS (told by Romin Teratol, Tzotzil, reprinted from Laughlin, *Of Cabbages and Kings*)

———————

This widespread Maya myth accounts for the origin of animals or, as here, just one kind of animal. In an old Quiché variant recorded in the Popol Vuh there are four brothers: two tree climbers, who become monkeys, and two survivors, who eventually become the sun and the moon. Here, again, there are two tree climbers—who in this case become pigs—but only one survivor, Sun, accompanied by his mother, Moon.

———————

It used to be that there were three suns, long ago, they say. There was no darkness. The suns took turns. It was always daytime because of the three suns, long ago. They traveled together. They went for a walk. They went to look for fruits. The two older brothers climbed a tree. The younger brother stayed at the foot of the tree. "Give me a fruit. I feel like eating one.

76

Throw one down to me," said the younger brother.

"Come on, climb up!" said the older brothers.

"I'm not going to climb up; throw them down here!" said the younger brother. They were thrown down to him, but just the chewings. He picked up the chewings. He made hind legs and forelegs for [the chewings]. He buried them at the foot of the tree.

Now they turned into an animal. They turned into a gopher. It gnawed the roots into pieces. The older brothers felt the tree moving now. "What are you doing, Xut?" asked the older brothers. "I'm not doing anything. Eat the fruit," said the younger brother.

The tree fell. Down came his older brothers. He went home. He arrived and told his mother, "Mother, give me six tortillas. I'm taking them, because I'm hungry," said Xut. He was given the tortillas. He went and grabbed his older brothers. Quickly he stuck noses and ears on his older brothers. He made their noses and ears out of the tortillas. He turned them into pigs. One, he turned into a peccary. The other, a domestic pig, he shut up in his house. The peccary ran off. It went to the woods.

He was only able to catch its tail. Its tail came off. It went. It fled into the woods. He drove the domestic pig to his house. "Mother, I've brought a pig. Give me food for it. The pig is hungry," said Xut.

"All right," said his mother. "Where are your older brothers?" asked his mother.

"I don't know. They must be having a good time someplace," Xut said.

"Ah!" she said. The first day she believed it. [Then] his mother cried and cried. Her tears flowed. That's why the moon's light is faint at night.

myth xvi : THE COURTSHIP OF SUN AND MOON (anonymous, Kekchi, adapted from Shaw, *According to Our Ancestors*)

*In Guatemala this story replaces The Childhood of Sun and Moon (myth xiv),
curiously retaining a key element: the stuffed deer carcass. In the Oaxaca tale
the two children use the carcass to fool their stepmother, while here it is used by
the young man to fool the woman he hopes to marry.*

I want to tell you a story that I heard in Poptún, Petén.

There was a man who was a king. The king had a daughter
who used to do her weaving in the patio.

There was a young man. The young man always passed there
with his blowgun as he went to hunt.

Every day when the young man passed by, he had a deer with
him. And when the girl saw this she said, "How many animals
that man gets! Let's see what I will do to him." And when the
girl washed her corn, she threw the corn water in the path.

Then when the man passed by and had a deer with him, he
fell on the corn water. When the deer hit the ground, it burst
and ashes fell out. Ashes were inside the skin.

Then the man was sad and embarrassed.

And he decided what to do. He turned himself into a hummingbird and went flitting around the flowers. The girl was
weaving in the patio. She saw how pretty that little animal was
as it sucked nectar from the flowers. She said to her father,
"Father, shoot that bird. I want it."

The father immediately came to shoot that animal, and the
little hummingbird fell to the ground. The girl took it and put
it by her side. "How pretty the colors of this little animal are,
the little hummingbird," she said. The girl kept it.

At night the girl slept in the kitchen [regarded as an ideal place
to sleep, because it is warmer and often more secure than other
parts of the house]. It was closed well because the king, her
father, locked it with a key.

When night came, the hummingbird regained consciousness.
And he stood up as a young man, and he began to make love
to the girl. He said to her, "Come with me, we will go away."

But the girl said, "How will we go? My father has locked the
door."

78

The young man said, "But if you want to, we can leave. We can go now if you want to," said the young man.

Then the girl was willing, but she said, "My father will find us with his glass."

The young man put *achiote* [an orange dye used for coloring food] on the glass so that the king could not see where they went.

The girl said, "But my father will kill us with his blowgun."

"Don't worry about that," the young man said. "I'll think of something to do. Let's go." And they went out through the keyhole.

Then they went off, went far away by the sea.

When the father woke up, he opened the door. He saw that his daughter wasn't there. He began to worry. "Where did my daughter go? Then it wasn't an animal that I killed. Perhaps it was a man."

He took his glass and put it to his eye. The *achiote* got into his eye, and that is how pinkeye started.

The king said, "I have hope with my blowgun." He found his gun, his blowgun, and he began to draw back his daughter with his blowgun, [sucking in his breath.]

And the young man, who was the sun, took some powdered chili, and when the king was drawing in on his blowgun, he threw it in the air. Then the king choked, and then he coughed—and that is how whooping cough started.

Then the king saw that he would not be able to get his daughter back. He talked to the volcano and said, "May my daughter be killed along with that man who took her."

And the volcano quickly flashed lightning. The young man — who was the sun—saw that the lightning was beginning to flash, and he knew that it was going to strike them. He quickly said to the turtle, "Turtle, may I borrow your shell?"

The turtle said, "Where would you enter? This house of mine is only big enough for me."

But the young man, the sun, had already snatched it. He put himself in the shell of the turtle. And when the lightning struck, the girl burst.

Everything landed in the water. Her blood all spilled out. Then the young man got out of the turtle shell. He saw her blood all spilled on top on the water. He said, "Now she is finished."

He hunted what to do. He borrowed the little animals that fly around the water, the dragonflies. He told them to gather up the blood. Some used bottles, some used skins, others used whatever they could to gather the blood.

So the little animals gathered up the blood. And when the little animals had finished, they said to him, "Here are your bottles." The young man, the sun, said, "Good." He gathered up all the bottles. He fixed them, he tied them.

He put them in his suitcase. He went off. He hunted a household. He said, "Please, I will leave my suitcase with you for two or three days, and then I will return to get it."

Then he left. The people took his suitcase and he left.

He didn't return for three weeks.

Two weeks after he had left the suitcase there, the little animals in his suitcase began to stir. With that the household began to be afraid of his suitcase. And the young man, the sun, still did not return.

And when he returned, the household was afraid. Immediately they said to him, "What is in your suitcase? How very much it is frightening us!"

And he said, "Oh, nothing. Maybe a rat is in my suitcase." And since the man already knew what was in his suitcase, he simply left, taking it with him.

And when he saw that he was far away from that house, he opened the bottles. There were little snakes that came out. Other creatures came out of the bottles and the skins and everything. And the one other place where the blood was he opened last, and he saw that nothing came out of it.

5

Journeys to the
Other World

myth xvii : THUNDER'S APPRENTICE (anonymous, Mam, translated
from the Spanish in Morales, "Cuentos mames")

---

*The story of the thunder god whose human helper makes foolish mistakes is
typical of the Maya area, though it is told as far north as the Distrito Federal
of Mexico (where the thunder spirits are "rain dwarfs" and their home is called
Tlalocan). Here, in a variant from the Mam of Guatemala, the scene is set in
the sky, the thunder spirit is "the lord of the clouds," and his helpers are "angels."*

They say it happened long ago, they say a man was carried off
by the lord of the clouds, who took him away to his home in the
sky, and when the man looked around, he saw angels. They were
just setting out with their capes, just beginning to run, starting
to thunder, and they made a cracking sound. In their hands they
carried a reflecting sword that flashes when rain falls, and makes
lightning. The noise of their capes is the storm, and when they
run, rain falls on the earth.

gl. Illustration #11 about here

81

The man saw what the angels did, and later he put on their capes and went out by himself. Rain came, but it was a pouring rain that never let up, a rain that made people sad and worried. When the angels heard the storm, they came to see who had caused it, and they saw the man running along. They caught him, and when they had taken him back to the house, they scolded him, and the rain let up, so it is said.

Another time, they say, the angels left the man at home to make supper, having first measured out the beans for him to cook. "Very well," he said. But after the angels had left, the man said to himself, "Ha! these beans are not enough. Better throw in a few more."

When the beans began to cook, oooh! they swelled and spread all over the floor. And to think he had said they would not be enough!

Then the angels came back and saw all the beans. "Did you throw in more beans?" they asked. "You had better go back where you came from." And the next thing the man knew, he was walking along just as he had been, before he had been carried away by the lord of the clouds.

myth xviii : THE DEAD WIFE (anonymous, Mískito, adapted from Conzemius, *Ethnographic Survey of the Miskito and Sumu Indians of Honduras and Nicaragua*)

In a Huichol version of this widespread myth, the husband who follows his deceased wife is allowed to bring her back to earth if he promises not to sleep with her; on the fifth day he breaks the prohibition, and she returns to the dead land—thus the true Orpheus tale, typical of the Indians of North America. South of the Mexican border, however, the story, as here, rarely includes the prohibition. Therefore it is better termed "The Dead Wife," rather than "The Orpheus Myth." In this Mískito variant notice the figure of the dog as ferryman, one of the most common motifs in the lore of Middle America.

A Mískito named Nakili had lost his wife, whom he loved very much. He went to her grave, and there, suddenly, he found himself in the presence of her *isiñni* [disembodied soul]. The soul, which was only about two feet high, announced that she was now starting on her journey to Mother Scorpion [the spirit of the hereafter].

The man wanted to go with her, but she told him that such a thing was out of the question, because he was still alive. But he insisted and would not be persuaded to stay behind. So they started out together, and as she led the way, she turned off onto a very narrow trail that he had never seen before.

They arrived at a place where there were many moths flying about. She was afraid of them and did not dare to proceed. But he chased them off, and they continued on their way.

After a while the trail led between two low pine trees, so close together that the wife could barely pass. The husband, being his normal size, was unable to squeeze through. Instead he walked around the two pine trees.

Continuing on, they came to a gorge spanned by a bridge the width of a human hair. Below was a huge pot of boiling water attended by *sikla* birds. The wife, small and light as she was, was able to walk over this narrow bridge. But Nakili did not find the distance across very great, and so he jumped it.

Then they arrived at a very large river, where there was a canoe paddled by a dog. This river was swarming with *bilim* [a tiny fish], which the soul thought were sharks. On the opposite shore they could see the country of Mother Scorpion, and everyone there appeared to be happy.

When the souls of those who had not led a righteous life tried to cross the river, the canoe would overturn, and the souls would be eaten by the *bilim*. The wife was ferried across safely by the dog, while the husband managed to swim alongside.

On the far shore they were received by Mother Scorpion, a very tall, stout woman with many breasts, to whom the inhabitants of the place came occasionally to suck like babies. She appeared to be angry at Nakili for having come, and she ordered him to go back to earth. He begged her to let him stay, because he loved his wife very much and did not wish to be separated from her.

She agreed finally that he could remain.

In this country no one had to work. There was plenty of excellent food and drink and no lack of amusements. But after staying for some time, Nakili longed to go back to earth in order to see his children again. Mother Scorpion allowed him to leave on condition that he would not return to the hereafter until he died. Then she put him in a huge bamboo rod, which she placed on the river. After a while he noticed high waves and realized that he was on the ocean, and finally a gigantic breaker threw him ashore, just in front of his own hut.

myth xix : THE BUZZARD HUSBAND (anonymous, Tzutujil, reprinted from Orellana, "Folk Literature of the Tzutujil Maya")

The Tzutujil variant given here is extraordinary in that the husband remains a buzzard. Usually he reverts to human form at the end of the story and returns to live with his wife (sometimes without her realizing that a switch has occurred). Another unusual variant comes from the Nahua of Durango, where the husband becomes a buzzard in order to search for his newly deceased wife, resulting in a myth in which two tale types, The Dead Wife and The Buzzard Husband, are combined.

A long time ago there was a man who was tired of his work. He was tired of going to the field and of bringing firewood and of all the work. He didn't want to work at all. He wanted a woman's life. He had a wife and children, but he didn't want to support them. He didn't work at all and just loafed around all day.

One day he went to the field and sat down on a stone. Then he saw a buzzard and said to himself, "This buzzard leads a good life because he doesn't have to do any work; he just flies around all day. He flies over the trees and over houses. I wish I could live like that buzzard for a little while." Then the buzzard came close to him, and he said to it, "Buzzard, I would like to speak to you for a moment. Come down."

"Okay," said the buzzard, and it immediately came down.

The man said to it, "I would like to turn into a buzzard because I like the kind of life you lead. You only fly through the air and don't have to work in the fields. I'm tired of working, and I don't want to work in the field anymore."

"Okay," the buzzard said. "If you want, you can become like me, but you have to eat the things I eat. I don't eat tortillas, only dead horses, cows, dogs, chickens, and pigs. We buzzards only eat dead things. It is okay if you can eat those things."

The man said, "Don't worry. I can do it. I can eat anything." Then the man jumped three times into the air, and then he turned into a buzzard and the buzzard turned into a man. They changed places.

The man who turned into a buzzard flew into the air; he was very happy. "This is the first time that I have found the good life," he said. He flew very high into the sky, flying over the trees, over valleys and over houses. He also flew over his own house. He saw his wife and children below. The buzzard who had changed into a man was there on the ground. When the man was tired of flying, he said, "I think I will go down because I am sure I can't eat the things buzzards eat. It would be impossible for me to eat dead things."

Slowly, he went down. When he was down, he began to jump, but he couldn't turn himself into a man again; he had become a buzzard permanently. "What am I going to do?" he said.

The buzzard who had turned into a man said to himself, "I think I'll go to the house of the man." When he got there, his body smelled bad and was putrid. He entered the house and the woman was there.

The woman said, "Why do you smell so bad? What have you been doing? I can't stand it. Get away from me. You aren't like you were before."

But it really wasn't her husband that she was talking to; she could not imagine that her husband had turned into a buzzard.

"But I have always smelled this way," he said.

Suddenly the woman saw a buzzard enter her house, and she was very surprised by this. "What does this mean? A buzzard has followed you here," she said.

The buzzard didn't want to leave and stayed flying around in

85

the house. The woman became very angry at the buzzard. It was terribly ugly to her. She went to get a stick and began to hit it. But it still didn't want to go away. The woman had no idea that it was her husband that she was hitting. Bang, bang went the blows on the buzzard. The woman said, "Horrible buzzard!"

And it did not go away. "What does this mean? A buzzard has never come into our house before."

Then the buzzard who had turned into a man said to the woman, "I am not really your husband; I am a buzzard. That's why I smelled so bad when I came in. That is your husband that you are hitting with the stick. He told me that he wanted very much to turn into a buzzard, and he turned into one." Then the woman began to cry a lot and was sad because her husband had turned into a buzzard. He wanted to become a man again, but he couldn't. He had become a buzzard permanently, and now he had to eat what buzzards eat.

myth xx : THE VISIT TO THE ANIMAL MASTER (told by Don Enrique, Chinantec, translated from the Spanish in Weitlaner, *Relatos, mitos y leyendas de la Chinantla*)

The lesson that game animals must be killed, not wounded and allowed to die unused, is a recurring feature of this widespread tale. In the variant given here, from the community of Valle Nacional in Oaxaca, the animal master wears the hat of a charro, or cowboy, reminiscent of the character called Big Hat, a spook well known in the folklore of southern Mexico and Guatemala.

There was a hunter who used to go out not far from the houses, shooting all the time, because in those days there was much game around Valle Nacional.

Once he was shooting when a man on a horse, with spurs and a big charro's hat, came along and asked him, "What are you doing here?"

The hunter said he was shooting game.

The man said, "Follow me."

And immediately, as in a dream, the hunter found himself in a cave. There the man showed him all the animals that he, the hunter, had wounded. There were pheasants with only one wing and many other hurt animals.

"Do you see these creatures that you have hurt? When you go out hunting, you must kill the animals. From now on, don't wound them, because if you do, my two dogs will come eat you up."

Then the hunter returned to the village and fell sick, and from that time on he never went hunting again.

PART THREE

Building

Mythologies

1

Myths in Sequence

An elementary step

One myth does not make a mythology. Stories in quantity are needed to authorize a people's customs, to illustrate the lessons that must be passed on to the young, and to answer the difficult questions "Where are we?" and "How did we get here?"

As is often the case, stories heard from grandparents and chance acquaintances can be saved up, then reeled off one by one around the hearth fire. This makes for good storytelling in the ordinary sense. But the term "mythology" implies a certain unity or interconnectedness that gives the stories added power. Often, though not always, the individual who understands how to put the myths together is no mere narrator but a religious specialist, who also knows songs, ceremonies, and other sacred lore.

The "basic" stories presented above, in Part Two, are among the native mythologist's raw materials. In addition, there are other, more unusual myths important to a particular community even if—or perhaps because—they are not told elsewhere. Spook stories, adventure stories, and other folktales may also be used, and in the process such everyday yarns may be elevated to the status of myth, at least locally.

The introduction of gods and the establishment of an imaginary universe are further features that help solidify a mythology, and these will be considered in the next chapter. For the moment, however, it may be sufficient to take a look at the simple, or perhaps not so simple, process of hooking one myth onto another—the elementary step in forming a connected body of narrative lore.

Paired myths

A typical variant of myth v, The Loss of the Ancients, provides a convenient starting point: in the days when the world was still dark, all animals could talk; but when the sun appeared for the first time, and the animal people watched it rise into the sky, they lost the power of speech forever.

Taking this unexceptional story, an unknown mythmaker whose version survives among the Nahua of northern Puebla has added several elements. The animals were farmers, we are told. They worked together with a boy who had a big cornfield; when the corn was ripe, they stored the kernels in a mountain; then, claiming that he had been "called away," the boy rose into the sky to become the sun, leaving the animals speechless, as we have seen.

With the storing of the corn kernels and the disappearance, or muting, of those who had put it away, the stage is set for the telling of myth ix (The Hidden Corn). And in fact the Nahua version continues with the story of the mountain filled with corn, the ant who brought it out, and the thunderbolts who broke open the mountain and brought it *all* out.

Looking over some of the other stories in Part Two, the casual reader might imagine that myth xii, which accounts for the origin of the sun (The Sun and the Fire) could be paired with myth xiii (How the Sun Was Named), as indeed it is in a Huichol version. Or myth xiv, which tells of the childhood of Sun and Moon, before they were transformed into heavenly bodies, could be coupled with The Sun and the Fire—as it is in a version from the Nahua of southern Puebla.

In each case the result is a creation story that offers the listener more to think about than if the paired myths were told separately. In this way, one begins to acquire a sense of the world's history.

The repeated myth

A striking feature of Middle American mythology is the tendency to combine variants of a single tale, The Loss of the Ancients, in order to create a myth of two, three, four, or five world ages. With each repetition the earth enters a new era. The best examples are from the Aztecs and from such Maya groups as the Quiché, the Yucatec, and the Tzotzil. The concept of world ages has also been reported for the Tarascans, the Totonac, and the Tarahumara.

According to a modern Yucatec version, the original people were the Adjusters, a race of dwarfs who lived in darkness and built the temples that are now in ruins. When the sun rose, these first people were turned to stone. A flood called "water over the earth" brought the first age to a close.

In the second age a people called the Offenders rose to power. Again the land was flooded.

Next the Yucatec appeared. But, as with the earlier races, their days were numbered, and their rule came to an end with a flood called "the immersing." Today, in the fourth age, Yucatan is populated by a mixture of all the races that existed previously.

Thus a typical Maya version of the repeated myth, with just four ages and a heavy emphasis on floods.

By contrast, in most Aztec versions the present age is the fifth in the series, and at the close of each of the previous ages not only are the people destroyed, but the sun as well. The sun we see today, therefore, is the fifth sun. As preserved in the sixteenth-century Annals of Cuauhtitlan, the story reads as follows:

"4 Water is the day sign of the first sun that there was in the beginning. And its name is Water Sun. All those who were created in its time were swept away by water. All the people turned into dragonfly nymphs and fish.

"4 Jaguar is the day sign of the second sun that there was, called Jaguar Sun. It happened that the sky collapsed then, and the sun did not continue. It happened at midday. Then there was darkness, and while it was dark, the people were eaten [by jaguars]. And giants were alive in the time of this one, and the old people say that their greeting was 'Don't fall!' because whoever fell would fall for good.

"4 Rain is the day sign of the third sun that there was, called Rain Sun. In the time of this one it happened that fire rained down, so that those who were there were burned. Also gravel rained down. They say that the gravel we find was strewn at this time. Also the lava stone boiled. And the various rocks that are red were deposited then.

"4 Wind is the day sign of the fourth sun, the Wind Sun. In its time, people were blown away by the wind, people were turned into monkeys. Those who remained, the monkey people, were scattered in the forest.

"4 Movement is the day sign of the fifth sun, called Movement Sun, because it moves along and follows its course. And from what the old people say, there will be earthquakes in its time, and famine, and because of this we will be destroyed."

The myth as given here, or a version very close to it, is preserved in the central portion of the great Aztec calendar stone, now in the National Museum of Anthropology in Mexico City. This famous sculpture dates from the reign of the Mexica king Axayacatl, who died in 1481, thirty-eight years before the arrival of the Spaniards.

Notice in the accompanying illustration that the central design has the overall form of a circle with four square knobs and two rounded knobs. This peculiar six-knobbed circle is a symbol for the day sign Movement, which, together with the four circlets flanking the rounded knobs, reads "4 Movement," the name of the fifth sun. (The complete name of each of the suns consists of a name and a number; this is also true of certain gods and ancient kings, who have names like 1 Reed or 8 Wind.)

In the square knob at lower right are four circlets and a human head sinking into water, which reads as the name of the first sun, 4 Water. Similarly, the remaining square knobs, reading counterclockwise, represent 4 Jaguar, 4 Wind, and 4 Rain, the second, fourth, and third suns.

Inside the circle is the face of the earth with its protruding tongue and its clawed hands resembling serpents' jaws extending into the two rounded knobs. The reader, or interpreter, of these symbols is evidently being reminded of the earthquake that will destroy the world when the time of the fifth sun has ended— just as in the version from the Annals of Cuauhtitlan, quoted above.

gl. Illustration #12 about here

Hence The Loss of the Ancients told four times, with an ominous fifth variant that foretells our own loss at an as yet undetermined moment in the future.

Graded sequences

An examination of old Quiché and Aztec versions of the myth of world ages suggests a theory of perfectability; that is, with each destruction and new creation the world becomes a little better.

According to the Quiché scheme, the first "people" were mere animals, who yielded to a second creation made of mud. Unable even to multiply, the flesh of mud gave way to a third race, carved from wood. Not until the fourth creation, however, were humans made from the proper material, which is corn.

95

In one of the Aztec versions, the first people are said to have used pine nuts as food. The food of the second age is not mentioned, but the third age provided something called *acicintli*, which may be translated either "water corn thing" or "not corn thing," presumably an inferior substitute for true corn. In the fourth age the people ate *cincocopi*, or wild corn, the *Euchlaena mexicana* of botanists, recognized as the ancestor of modern maize.

Another of the Aztec versions—the one from the Annals of Cuauhtitlan, fully quoted above—has the first people changing into dragonfly nymphs and fish. The fourth people became monkeys; and the fifth people, we must assume, are completely human. So here again we have a kind of evolutionary sequence, albeit with gaps.

Myth time

Even if stories are not actually linked together, they may be thought of as belonging in a certain sequence nonetheless. Usually the ordering principle is quite simple: there is a time of creation, an ancient time, when anything can happen, and a more recent time, when marvels are restricted.

Among the Tzotzil of Chamula, however, a most unusual discovery was made in the 1960s by the Chamula specialist Gary Gossen, who found that storytellers put the "ancient" narratives (as opposed to the "recent" ones) into three separate categories, according to the theory of world ages. In other words, some of the old stories tell of events that occurred during the first creation, before the initial loss of the ancients. Others are set during the second or third creations, while "recent" stories are from the fourth, or present, creation.

Gossen reports a collection of 92 "ancient" stories divided among the first three creations, as follows:

First creation: 47 stories, including The Man of Crops (3 variants), The Loss of the Ancients (8 variants), Sun and His Brothers

(2 variants), Adam and Eve, life of Christ, deeds of God the Father, deeds of Christ, and saints' legends.

Second creation: 23 stories, including The Loss of the Ancients (2 variants), The Flood Myth (combined with The Loss of the Ancients), Sun and His Brothers, The Dead Wife, The Buzzard Husband, and saints' legends.

Third creation: 22 stories, including The Loss of the Ancients, The Dead Wife, The Visit to the Animal Master, a European fairy tale called The Girl as Helper in the Hero's Flight, and animal trickster tales borrowed from Europeans.

It is understandable that The Loss of the Ancients would occur in all three categories, since the myth must be told three times in order to get the world into the fourth age. But it is puzzling to find both The Dead Wife and Sun and His Brothers appearing in more than one time level. The reason, apparently, is that the myths were collected from six narrators, each with a somewhat different idea of the overall scheme.

It seems to be generally recognized, though, that the life of Christ and the myths about God the father belong in the earliest period, as does The Man of Crops (whom the people of Chamula identify with Jesus).

The placement of a European fairy tale and European trickster tales in the time of the third creation indicates the difficulty in getting a precise definition of myth. What seem as folktales to some may be myths to others. Nevertheless, the Chamula have a mythological system about which there is some agreement.

The Chamula scheme stands in contrast to the sequencing found in most other Indian cultures, where, as mentioned, myths are simply assigned to a generalized myth time, which may be signaled by a comment to the effect that such and such occurred when rocks could talk (Mixtec) or before the fall of the ocean tree (Bribri). The most common when-it-was formulas may be summarized briefly:

When the world was still dark (Aztec, Bribri, Mixtec, Pipil, Tarahumara, etc.). The appearance of light is the most familiar time marker in Middle American mythology. The reference is to the sun, rarely the moon, occasionally Christ, whose birth is mystically identified with the first sunrise.

When animals were people (Bribri, Lenca, Popoluca, etc.). The human attributes of animals are simply taken for granted in most tribal traditions. But sometimes, as among the Popoluca, a narrator may actually start off by saying, "Once upon a time when animals could speak."

When trees talked (Ixil, Lenca, Zapotec). Trees talked in the beginning, say the Lenca. The Ixil idea is that trees cried out and bled if someone attempted to cut them. According to the Zapotec, they wept when the world flood began. Tzotzil say that grass could talk. A related belief, held by the Yaqui, is that a talking tree of the ancient time foretold the future.

When the earth was soft (Boruca, Bribri, Mazatec, Nahua of Durango, Pipil, Quiché, Tarahumara, Tzotzil, Yucatec, Zapotec). A typical idea is that the earth was soft after the great flood; eventually it dried out, or hardened. The Boruca speak of a time when rocks were "like clay." In many mythologies, unusual rock formations are explained on the theory that they were molded or imprinted by the ancients.

When the sun was close (Tarahumara). Formerly the sun was so close that rocks on the earth were molten. Stars were close, according to a related Mazatec belief—so close that people could throw stones at them.

Often two or more of these ideas will be used together, as in the words of the Pipil storyteller who begins, "In the days when there was not yet a moon, all was in darkness. And all the rocks were soft."

The folkloric creation tale

The world is in darkness, people have no fire, there is no corn, the earth is perpetually abused, the dead land is different from the world of the living. Such are the themes that Europeans recognize as mythic and that form the basis for Indian stories called "ancient" or "delicate."

Folkloric tales are more personal, focusing not on elemental creation but on some aspect of family conflict or drama: two children are lost, a wife is unfaithful to her husband, a young woman wishes to marry, brothers detest each other, a boy resents his father, a man feels trapped by his clinging wife, a father desires his daughter.

As attested by the stately creation epics of the Aztecs, mythology can flourish with little or no help from the folkloric tale. It simply strings together one myth after another.

But there is a different approach, more typical of smaller cultures, whether of North, South, or Middle America, that tends to proceed from the personal. That is, it begins with the folktale, sets the primal scene as a family drama, then moves into myth.

On a modest scale we may see how this works in such basic Middle American stories as The Childhood of Sun and Moon (myth xiv), which opens with the lost children and their resentment of the stepfather; or Sun and His Brothers (myth xv), where a family conflict leads to the origin of animals; or The Courtship of Sun and Moon (myth xvi), with its marriage-minded young woman and overprotective father.

A large-scale example, built out of four separate stories, is provided by the important creation cycle of the Pipil of El Salvador, accounting for the origin of rain and the establishment of agriculture. The cycle, or group of stories, comprises two folktales and two myths in the sequence folktale-myth-folktale-myth, put together in such a way that the problem of a faithless yet clinging wife is resolved in the origin of rain; and the murderous contest between an old woman's lover and her little boys leads to the discovery of corn.

One may ask, How can essential features of the environment be regarded as an outgrowth of personal relationships? The very act of articulating such a question, not to mention the agony of answering it, belongs to the European science of mythology. Native thinkers prefer to take the material at face value, working it into new combinations, repeating it, varying it, until its strangeness disappears.

Let us suspend disbelief, therefore, and experience the whole Pipil epic as a construction of spare parts.

The first of the four "parts" is a standard spook story, well known among the Tzotzil of Zinacantán, with a single variant reported from the Kekchi of Belize. It may be called The Bodiless Wife.

The second story is an unusual myth of the origin of heroes from the fruit of a parental tree. The only similar tale, among those that have been reported, is the account of the skull-fruit that fathers the twin heroes of the Popol Vuh.

The third story is the folktale that will here be called Old Woman's Lover. It is a variant of the main episode of The Childhood of Sun and Moon (myth xiv), and it is told as a separate tale among the Mopan and the Kekchi.

Finally, the fourth of these spare parts is the familiar Hidden Corn in a version reminiscent of the Mopan variant given in Part Two as myth ix.

The sequence opens with the tale of the woman whose head goes wandering at night, while her body remains in bed next to her husband. Deceived, the man suspects nothing until a neighbor advises him, "Watch after your wife. She goes out at night to sleep with someone else."

The husband watched and saw that it was true. The head, the arms, and the legs detached themselves from the body and went out. Following the further advice of the neighbor, the man rubbed salt on the severed joints and waited to see what would happen. In the words of the narrator:

"When the head came back, it tried to clamp on. Not good! It tried again. Not good! It fell off, came back and tried again. Not good! "Then the arms came. Not good!

Then the legs came. Not good! Then the head said, 'Get up!' 'What do you want?' 'Get up. I want you to tell me why you did such a miserable thing. And to keep you from doing it again, I'm going to clamp onto you!' Then she fastened herself to her husband.

100

"From then on, he had two heads. When he went off to work, his wife's head went with him. When he ate, she ate, too.

"And when she defecated, it was through her husband's anus. And when she urinated, it was through her husband's penis.

"When it was time to sleep, she detached herself from her husband and lay beside him, chatting aimiably.

"But at his slightest move, she was on the alert. He could not get away from her."

One day, while they are walking in the woods, the man offers to climb a sapodilla tree in order to pick fruits for his wife. Tempted, she detaches herself and waits patiently on the ground. Up in the tree, while searching for ripe fruits, the man picks a green one and throws it away. The hard fruit hits a deer that happens to be nearby, causing it to jump; and the wife, thinking it is her husband trying to get away, pursues the deer and clamps onto its rump. As the animal runs through the brush, the woman's head is lacerated by brambles, dies, and falls off.

Feeling guilty, the husband goes to confession and asks the priest what he ought to do. The advice he receives leads into the epic's second part, the myth that accounts for the birth of the rain children.

On orders from the priest, the man finds his wife's head and buries it. Day after day he watches the grave, until a gourd-fruit tree sprouts up.

At first the sapling just oozes a little blood. As it grows larger, it bears fruit. Then a noise of scuffling can be heard from the gourd-fruits, and as they ripen and burst, little boys begin dropping out of the tree.

The man picks up the children, dresses them in tiny pieces of cloth he has bought in the village, and brings them home to be raised by his old mother—the mother of the folktale Old Woman's Lover. Thus the epic moves smoothly into its third part.

Under the old woman's care the little ones grow rapidly. In no time they are bringing home game, which the mother regularly cooks for their supper.

When the woman takes a giant as her lover, the giant has to

101

be fed, too.

One day the boys come home from hunting so weary that they fall asleep immediately, all but the littlest, who stays awake and sees the giant eating up their food. The giant saves only a tiny amount, which he smears on the lips of the sleeping boys.

When the boys wake up hungry, the mother says, "You've eaten already."

"Then why are we hungry?"

"Figure it out for yourselves!"

Running their tongues over their lips, they begin to believe they have really eaten. But the littlest, who had stayed awake, explains that the old woman's lover tricked them and took all the food for himself.

Then the boys dig a pitfall and line it with sharpened stakes. Next time the giant comes along, he falls in and is killed. The children cut off his genital member, bring it home to the old woman as a roast, and after she has eaten it, the littlest challenges her to a urinating contest. He sends his stream arching up over the house, while the old woman's urine "just took the low road, running along beside her bottom."

After that the boys run off, as the littlest remarks, "We'll laugh forever. You ate your lover's penis."

"You man!" cries the woman. "Is that what you did? Don't ever do it again!"

The boys travel far. As they are going along, they notice a bird eating a strange kernel—the opening motif of The Hidden Corn (myth ix), which forms the epic's fourth and final part.

When the boys see that the bird gets the corn from inside a mountain, they decide to break it open. Putting their plan into action, they make a little raincloud, which rises into the sky and sends down a thunderbolt. But after repeated tries, the mountain is still intact.

Then the littlest boy steps up, makes a storm, and hurls a thunderbolt that splits the mountain with a single stroke, causing so much corn to pour out that it buries him completely. Before he can get free, his brothers take all the largest ears for themselves.

The foolish brothers eat their corn, while the littlest plants and irrigates his fields. Watching to see how he does it, they mend their ways and ask for seed corn. "I shouldn't do it," says the littlest, "but I'll give you some anyway. Go now, and plant it. And in eight days you'll see the corn coming up. Go! And don't come back, don't ever come back!"

Thus the epic tale begins as it ends, with the kind of interpersonal conflict that belongs to fiction and folklore but not necessarily mythology. Yet the story does more than illuminate life; it establishes life's sources, as does all good myth.

In the words of Leonhard Schultze Jena, the German linguist who collected the tale and prepared a grammar of the Pipil language, "Pipil thought focuses on four things: crops, which the people transform into flesh and blood; earth, from which the crops draw strength; water, without which there can be no life; and the heavenly bodies that rule the world."

Although the "heavenly bodies" do not play a role here, the epic of the rain boys, for all its human interest, does indeed focus on crops and on water (or "rain children")—in short, the fundamental needs of humanity.

2

Gods and the Ordering of Space

A province of its own

As used in this book, the term "mythology" means either a group of creation stories or the study of these stories. The category may be stretched to include certain tales of otherworldly journeys, hero tales, and semihistorical legends. But it does not include such elements of sacred lore as the names and characteristics of gods, or beliefs about the structure of the sky, the earth, and the underworld.

Nevertheless, the subject of spirit powers and world pictures does relate to Indian myth, since gods may assume leading roles in the narratives, and the action may take place in a region of the universe inaccessible to ordinary eyesight.

The following few pages will attempt a broad view of these religious and philosophical ideas. But it should be kept in mind that this is a vast province of its own, making connection with myth only at selected points. The elaborate world pictures created by Aztec artists contain few features ever mentioned in myth, and for the most part the innumerable gods of the Maya,

104

the Aztecs, the Zapotecs, the Huichol, and others are simply names without stories.

The principal powers

Fittingly, for a region dedicated to agriculture, the typical gods of Mesoamerica are rain spirits and earth spirits. Sun and Moon, widely recognized, are perhaps more prominent today than they were formerly, having become merged with the new spirits God, Christ, and the Virgin. Other deities, including lords of the underworld and spirits of corn, salt, and fire, are locally important. But for the territory as a whole, earth and rain powers deserve first mention.

In Aztec and Maya traditions, the rain lord is a master spirit, attended by several or many helpers. His name in the Aztec language is Tlaloc, and his helpers are *tlaloque* (tlalocs). Among the Yucatec Maya, Chac and the chacs are recognized; the Mopan speak of Mam and the mams.

In some traditions, as with the Pipil, the master may be missing, and we simply find "rain children," or "rain boys." Modern Nahua consider these numerous spirits to be dwarfs, or little people. The Zoque say that they are very old but look like boys. The closer one gets to Guatemala, the more likely they are to be gods of thunder and lightning as well as of rain. Thunder's Apprentice (myth xvii) is a story about such spirits. Another is The Hidden Corn (myth ix).

Invariably the rain spirit is male, though he may have a wife who shares his dominion over the waters. The spirit of the earth, on the other hand, is often feminine. Among the Aztecs she was said to have been a hungry woman with mouths at every joint of her body. According to the modern Jicaque, the cracks in the earth's surface are her thirsty mouths. These ideas, however, often amount to mere personifications rather than actual deities. Why the Earth Eats the Dead (myth iii), for instance, is a story not of a deity but of the personified earth.

105

Spirits that may be recognized as full-fledged earth goddesses include Coatlicue (Snake Skirt) of the Aztecs, the Huichol goddess Nakawé (also called Grandmother Growth), and the twelve old women known to the Totonac as owners of the soil.

In Oaxaca and in the Maya area, earth deities are masculine. Here they are thought of not as *representing* the soil but as *owning* it. Often such a spirit is called Lord of the Hills, or Lord of the Hills and Valleys, and usually these male spirits are also animal masters; that is, they control the supply of game and can withhold animals from unworthy hunters. The Visit to the Animal Master (myth xx) makes reference to this class of deity.

Additional spirits include the lords of the dead, which played a significant role in the elaborate religions of the Aztecs and the ancient Maya, also fire lords, important in old Aztec and in modern Huichol traditions. Corn gods, wine gods, salt goddesses, and countless others are known from both ancient and contemporary lore.

Is there a supreme deity? Perhaps so, judging from reports that have accumulated since the sixteenth century. In early colonial days, Aztecs spoke of Ipalnemohuani (Life Giver), also called Tloque Nahuaque (Ever Present Ever Near), while the Yucatec are said to have worshipped Hunab Ku (Only Spirit), also called Itzamná. More recently, there have been reports of Itom Ae (Our Mother) for the Yaqui, Onorúame (He Who Is Father) for the Tarahumara, and the familiar Sibú for the Bribri and Cabécar — to mention only a few.

The question is whether these deities, evidently supreme, were somewhat less so in pre-Conquest times.

What is quite certain is that the old religions often recognize a primal pair; and, in addition, there is a tendency to form myths around the figure of an active creator, or world shaper. The first of these concepts is of a passive "mother" and "father" who merely plan creation or give birth to other gods. Examples have been reported from the Aztecs, the Chinantec, the Tlapanec, the Zoque, and other groups in the Aztec-Maya area. The second idea, more prominent, is of a busy spirit who takes charge or

106

interferes in creative activities, for example, Quetzalcoatl of the Aztecs.

Typically, the active spirit has a companion or adversary, who helps or hinders his work. So Quetzalcoatl has Tezcatlipoca. Sibú has the evil Sorkura. Among the Lacandon the two are Hachakyom and Kisin. Tarahumara speak of Elder Brother and Younger Brother.

Over the years these active creators have lost ground. Although they hold their own in favored localities, they have been forgotten elsewhere, or they have been replaced by God and the Devil.

At the same time, the primal "mother" and "father" have been superseded by God and the Virgin, or Dios and Santa María, to use the Spanish terms—and these in turn are now identified with the sun and the moon. The Mayo of northwest Mexico say that the stars are the children of this heavenly pair. In some cases, Christ is the sun. Or, as among the Southern Tepehuan, God is Sun, and Christ is Moon. Such sun-and-moon families are typical of modern folk religions throughout Mexico and Guatemala.

Quetzalcoatl and Tezcatlipoca

The most famous of the paired creators—the active ones, not the mother-father spirits—are the Aztec gods Quetzalcoatl (Plumed Serpent) and Tezcatlipoca (Smoking Mirror). The myths in which they appear give proof of their varied activities:

Why the Earth Eats the Dead (myth iii). To make earth, Quetzalcoatl and Tezcatlipoca dragged the hungry woman out of the sky and spread her body over the ocean. In the process they treated her roughly. Hoping to soothe her, the other gods descended and made forests, flowers, valleys, and other pleasant features on her surface. Nevertheless, to this day she craves human hearts and wishes to be watered with human blood.

The Loss of the Ancients (myth v). When the gods had made the first sun, Tezcatlipoca stole it, tied it around his middle, then rose to the sky. Quetzalcoatl followed him with a big stick and knocked him back to earth, where he became the jaguar that ate the first people.

The Flood Myth (myth vi). Tezcatlipoca helped one couple seal themselves in a watertight boat. After the flood had subsided, the two survivors offended the gods by roasting a fish, and Tezcatlipoca, to punish them, came back and changed them into dogs.

The Hidden Corn (myth ix). Quetzalcoatl noticed an ant carrying a corn kernel. He himself became an ant, followed the other ant into a mountain, and discovered that its insides were filled with corn.

The origin of flowers. Quetzalcoatl spilled semen, which gave birth to a bat. The animal then flew to Xochiquetzal, goddess of love, and bit off the "piece of flesh" that she had within her genitals. The bat brought this to the gods, who transformed it into flowers.

The origin of music. A man in search of Tezcatlipoca was instructed to fetch musicians from the sun. The man did so, and in this way music, born in the sky, was brought to earth.

How the sky was raised. During the final flood of the ancient time, the sky itself fell to earth. Quetzalcoatl and Tezcatlipoca then changed themselves into two trees that kept growing taller, pushing the sky back to its normal position. Leaving the trees in place, one at each end of the earth, the two deities climbed over the edge of the sky, met at the center of the Milky Way, and became "the lords of heaven and of the stars."

Despite this last myth, it is hard to be certain that either Quetzalcoatl or Tezcatlipoca should be called the supreme deity of Aztec religion. Yet the names Life Giver and Ever Present Ever Near, used by Christian Aztecs to mean God the Father, did originally apply to one or both of these two rival spirits; and some early observers were prepared to state that for the Mexica Aztecs, at least, Tezcatlipoca had been the preeminent power.

Gods in groups

Although Quetzalcoatl and Tezcatlipoca are the principal actors in the myths that have been summarized above, it will be noticed that "the gods," as a group, play a role as well. We hear that "the gods" were offended, or that they made the first sun, or that they put the finishing touches on the creation of flowers.

Committees of gods are typical of the lore—especially the ancient lore—of central Mexico, Oaxaca, and the Maya area. Sometimes "the gods" are not identified and their number is indefinite. But not always.

In a report from the Trique of southern Oaxaca, a group of exactly nine gods is said to have issued from a father deity, who orders them to make the world. These sons are deities of earth, sun, moon, light, water, air, frost, death, and the underworld.

The earth god begins, but creates only slime. To dry it, the god of light steps forward. But the earth begins to burn. So Water and Frost take over, creating hills, valleys, rivers, and forests. Yet they work too hard, causing a flood, and the god of air has to be summoned to undo the damage. In this way the world is created through a process of alternation between gods of the wet and gods of the dry.

A group of exactly nine gods was also recognized by the Aztecs and by the ancient Maya. These deities were said to have been lords of the night or lords of the underworld. They were balanced by a group of thirteen deities, representing either the day or the sky world. Presumably both groups of spirits were related to ancient calendrical systems, which were based on a "week" of nine days or, more commonly, thirteen days.

In the twentieth century, groups of nine gods were still to be found in certain Zapotec communities. Here again, as among the Trique, they were divided between wet and dry. Some, like the rain god, belonged to the rainy season; others, including the god of harvests, belonged to the dry.

Seasonal divisions have also been reported for the Huichol, where it is said that Grandmother Growth belongs to the wet season, while the deities of the dry season include the fire god and the sun.

109

Indeed, one investigator has found that all Huichol mythology is organized along seasonal lines: there is the wet-season cycle and the dry-season cycle. The Flood Myth (myth vi), Corn Woman's Marriage (myth x), and The Dead Wife (myth xviii) fit into the wet-season epic, while Opossum Steals Fire (myth iv) and How the Sun Was Named (myth xiii), naturally, are among the dry-season stories.

Quartering

It was mentioned above that when Quetzalcoatl and Tezcatlipoca shaped the hungry woman, they treated her roughly. The original text tells precisely what they did: "They said to each other, 'The earth must be made,' and with these words they changed into two large snakes, one of which took hold of the goddess from her right hand down to her left foot, the other from her left hand down to her right foot, [thus forming a cross.]"

With reference to a similar procedure, the Popol Vuh of the Quiché Maya reveals that the old traditions told "how all the sky and the earth were formed, how it was formed and divided into four parts, how . . . the measuring cord was brought, and it was stretched in the sky and over the earth, on the four angles, on the four corners."

In an unusual variant from the Guaymí, it is said that the hungry woman clashed with her two sons, who tried to get rid of her by throwing her first to the east, then to the west, then to the south (the fourth direction, north, is not mentioned); and because she kept coming back, they finally threw her into the earth, and there she remained.

According to the Bribri, when the great tree fell, giving the earth its present form, God hoped it would fall on Old Woman Hunger and kill her; but she survived. Then he sent the deer with a measuring cord to divide the world into four quarters (east, south, west, and north). The deer was so swift that it accomplished its task in just four leaps.

In another Bribri version, four new trees spring up, and the deer, which has been assigned to "take charge" of them, makes a complete circuit of the new earth, again in four leaps.

In all cases, the underlying idea is that the world must be divided into four equal parts.

Belief in a "world picture" that includes four trees is even more common than the idea of quartering with snakes or cords. Huichol say that the four trees hold up the earth. In most other traditions, however, the trees are in the space between earth and sky.

In some religions, as with the Kekchi, there is not just one earth lord, but four. There may also be four rain gods, as in Ixil lore. Four special animals, four birds, four mountains, or four colors may also be recognized, one for each of the four quarters.

The accompanying illustration, from the Aztec codex known as the Fejérváry-Mayer, shows one artist's conception of the overall design. In this picture each of the four directions has its tree, surmounted by its particular bird. Notice that the nine gods are also present, one in the center and two for each of the quarters. The central deity is Xiuhteuctli, the fire god, regarded by the Aztecs as the oldest of all the spirits.

World levels and world houses

Most native people in Middle America imagine the universe as a structure of at least three layers: underworld, earth's surface, and sky world. This is an independent belief, unconnected to the idea of world quarters.

gl. Illustration #13 about here

Among the Tarahumara it is said that there are seven levels, earth's surface being the fourth, or middle, of these. For the Jicaque, as well as for the modern Yucatec, there are seven skies above the earth and two or more underworlds beneath it, making a total of at least ten layers.

For the Aztecs there were thirteen upper and nine lower levels. But the skies were counted upward starting with earth's surface, making an actual total of only twelve; and the lower levels were counted downward in the same manner, so that there were really only eight. The highest of the Aztec heavens was called Omeyocan (Two Place), inhabited by the primal pair, Ometeuctli (Two Lord) and Omecihuatl (Two Woman).

Thirteen sky levels have also been reported for the Tzotzil and the ancient Yucatec, although here the levels are arranged in a kind of imaginary pyramid, with six ascending steps, or levels, on each side and a step-sized platform at the apex. Overall, however, the Tzotzil think of the universe as a cube, with the souls of the dead in its lower portion, covered over by the square that forms earth's surface.

Similarly, the late archaeologist J. E. S. Thompson found evidence to suggest that the ancient Yucatec imagined the universe as a rectangular box, a kind of house, framed by the stringlike body of the figure known to more recent Mayanists as the Celestial Monster, or Cosmic Monster.

It is well attested that the Bribri of Costa Rica consider the universe to be the house of Sibú, the supreme deity. In this case, one must visualize the old-style Bribri house with its circular floor plan and enormous cone-shaped loft; the earth's surface is the "floor." (A variant idea from the Guaymí is that the floor of the cosmic dwelling is at the bottom of the underworld, while the floor of its loft forms the earth's surface.)

Bribri say that the stars of the Pleiades, the constellation popularly known in English as the Seven Sisters, are the tips of Sibú's roof poles. Inevitably, this "house" of Sibú is the locale of myths. For instance, when the soil-forming bat returns from the underworld, after drinking the blood of the infant earth, Sibú finds him hanging from the "clear sky" of the world house (myth iii). Later, when the soil has been deposited and the great ocean-forming tree has sprung up, it grows so tall that it threatens to break through the "roof." It is to preserve the house that the tree has to be cut down (myth viii: The Tree and the Flood).

Day sky, night sky

Tarahumara and Jicaque say that the sun, during the day, travels in the uppermost level of the sky. Aztecs placed the sun in the fourth heaven, while the stars rode along in the third. According to modern Tzotzil, at least in one community, sun, moon, and stars belong to the second layer. Virtually all Middle American traditions agree, however, that the sun at night makes its way through the underworld, traveling west to east.

But it was not always so. According to a Kekchi mythmaker, in the old days Lord Sun "placed a mirror in the center of the sky, and every morning he used to start out from his home in the east and travel till he got to the center. Then he used to turn back home, but the mirror reflected his light, and it appeared as though he were continuing his journey."

At least one Aztec mythmaker evidently believed that the situation had never been corrected. His testimony was that the sun "rises in the morning, traverses till midday, and then returns to the east in order to start again next day, and what is visible from noon till sunset is its brightness, and not the sun itself, and at night it neither shows itself nor has motion."

The fact remains that the earth is in darkness at night, or nearly so.

After sunset, according to the Tepehua, the stars take over the sun's role as protector. Their task is essential because stones turn into jaguars when the sun is absent and threaten to devour people. To keep the earth safe, stars shoot arrows at the jaguars—hence the explanation of shooting stars, or meteors.

Myths that account for the origin of the sun (and the moon) are standardized in Middle America, and typical variants may be read in section four of Part Two, above. Star myths, on the other hand, are extremely diverse, with little evidence of regional patterning.

113

A story of the Lacandon explains that the god Hachakyom planted stars by scattering grains of sand. Today these points of light are the roots of trees that grow in the sky world. When a tree falls in the forest of Hachakyom, it is seen below as a meteor.

According to Jicaque tradition, when the ancients were banished from the earth's surface, they rose into the sky and became stars. Since they continually eat the fruits that ripen in the sky forests, they are always defecating; and their droppings, which may be seen as meteors, are the seeds that sow the forests of earth.

An even more unusual myth, reported from the Cabécar, has it that when the great Sibú was building his house, he found himself without vines to lash the timbers. He therefore sent a work party to bring back a whisker from the serpent who lives in the east. Twenty-five men were needed to roll up this whisker and carry it home. When Sibú received it, he tied his house, and each knot formed a star.

Afterworlds

A portion of the universe, preferably far removed from the living, is reserved for the souls of the dead. It is located either in the highest heaven or in the lowest layer of the underworld. Or it may lie at the extremity of one of the four directions.

According to the Bribri, the dead land is below the place where the sun comes up. The Seri, taking an opposite view, believe it is somewhat to the north of the point where the sun goes down. In Mískito lore, it is at the end of the Milky Way.

Yucatec who believe in seven sky levels say there is a hole in the center of each of the layers. A ceiba tree, growing at the center of the earth, extends upward through the holes, and it is by climbing this tree that the souls of the dead progress from level to level, eventually reaching the uppermost heaven, where the God of Christianity lives.

Aztecs used to say that the soul's destination was the lowest of the nine (or eight) underworlds. At each level there was a danger that had to be passed. According to one source, the obstacles were as listed here:

1. *Apanohuayan* (water-crossing place), where souls are ferried across a river on the back of a dog

2. *Tepetlimonamiquiyan* (where mountains come together), the obstacle well known to comparative mythologists, recalling the Symplegades, or clashing rocks, of ancient Greek lore

3. *Itztepetl* (knife mountain)

4. *Ehecayan* (wind place)

5. *Pacoecoetlacaya* (should be *Pancuecuetlacayan?*), probably referring to the banners (*pantli*) that symbolized human sacrifice

6. *Temiminaloyan* (place where one is repeatedly shot with arrows)

7. *Teocoylqualoya* (probably should be *Teyollocualoyan*, place where one's heart is eaten)

8. *Iz Mictlan, Apochcalocan* ("this is the dead land, the place without chimneys"), where there is no outlet whatsoever, no escape

Even so, there is no insurance against the return of the dead. Aztecs believed that dead warriors, if they had been killed in battle, could return as birds or butterflies. Tarahumara believe that the soul in some cases may return to the earth's surface in the form of a moth, called the ancestor moth. Eventually, though, it falls into a fire and is consumed.

Moths and butterflies, apparently representing dead souls, are also found in the lore of the Bribri and the Mískito. Chinantec say that the souls are converted to butterflies—but, fortunately, they are promptly eaten by birds.

It is clear enough that the obstacle course, as listed above, is to prevent the ghost from coming back to harm the living. According to the Lacandon, the obstacles are illusions that merely deceive the souls. For instance, the river that one must pass is really nothing more than the tears of one's grieving relatives. But the dead person sees it as a barrier that, once crossed, cannot be crossed again.

115

The river, or other body of water, generally guarded by a dog, is the most consistent feature of this funereal lore. Often the dog is envisioned as black (Aztec, Chinantec, Mazatec, Nahua, Popoluca, Tarascan, Tzotzil). Sometimes, as among the Rama of Nicaragua, it is said that the dog ferries only the virtuous, while devouring the wicked. Seri say that the dog guards a pot of boiling water, to which the wicked are consigned; only the innocent pass unscathed.

For reasons that should be apparent, dogs are treated with respect. A Lacandon story, for instance, tells how a dead man who had mistreated his dog was refused passage to the afterworld. Tarascans say that a black dog, if abused, will complain to God. J. E. S. Thompson has written that ancient Maya tombs "have yielded skeletons of dogs and, in one instance, a flint carving of an alert dog." Presumably the burials were prepared in this manner in order to assist the dead in their difficult journey.

One of the mysteries of Mesoamerican lore is that the dead land is not necessarily one place. Its location may vary according to the cause of death. In central Mexico especially, there is a tendency to regard the afterworld as three places. Among the modern Nahua these are (1) the paradise of the rain dwarfs, where drowning victims go; (2) the sky world, for soldiers killed in battle and women who have died in childbirth; and (3) the regular underworld, for everyone else.

But not quite everyone. Children who die at a tender age have a destiny all their own. In Aztec belief they go to a special paradise where they sit beneath a tree of human breasts, catching the milk in their mouths. The modern Tzotzil of Zinacantán have the same idea: the babies sit with their mouths opened wide to catch the drops of milk as they fall. Tzotzil of Chamula say that the infants are placed within the tree, where they can actually suckle. The similar Mískito belief is that the dead go to Mother Scorpion, described as a "tall" woman with many breasts (see Part Two, myth xviii); and it is from Mother Scorpion that souls are sent to earth as newborn children.

Whether envisioned as a house, a cube, a pyramid, or a cakelike structure of many layers, the universe has ample room for both the living and the dead, as well as the supernatural. Though in the more limited representations it may seem no more than a quartered pie, the details can always be filled in, or the whole can be expanded, to reveal additional chambers, accommodating all the powers that lie beyond ordinary experience.

3

Adventures
of the Hero

"Before he became sacred"

The figure of the hero helps to bridge the gap between myth and history. Unlike the gods, he is usually a man who has lived on earth, often with a definite life span that begins with his birth and ends with his death or disappearance.

Nevertheless, heroes can become gods, and vice versa. Quetzalcoatl is a major deity of the Aztecs, but in some stories he is an earthly hero. The same is true of the Maya god Itzamná; and in modern lore, Christ is usually the tragic hero pursued and crucified, yet he sometimes fills the role of God the Creator.

Among the Huichol, the important god of hunting known as Elder Brother Deer Tail may also be called Kauyumari (Makes People Crazy), of whom trickster stories are told. In the latter case, the narrator will add, "Well, of course that happened in those days before he became sacred."

The heroic child

The legendary hero of Mexico and Central America has many guises and hybrid forms. Yet two fundamental types may be distinguished. One is the wise instructor, typically a mature man who appears in a particular community, accomplishes his mission, then withdraws. The other is a defiant little boy born on earth in a miraculous manner.

Of the defiant children, the most famous is the Aztec hero Huitzilopochtli (Hummingbird Left Hand), deified as the tribal spirit of the Mexica Aztecs. The Mexica placed his shrine on their highest pyramid, next to the rain god.

Huitzilopochtli's birth is supposed to have occurred at the summit of a certain Snake Mountain, not far from the old Toltec capital of Tula. The hero's mother, it seems, had been sweeping one day when she noticed a tuft of feathers, which she picked up and tucked into her skirt. From this she conceived.

But the woman—whose name, Coatlicue (Snake Skirt), is the same as that of the earth goddess—already had four hundred sons, also a warlike daughter who led the entire pack. Hearing that their mother was pregnant again, these older children flew into a rage and plotted to kill the newborn.

Just as Coatlicue was about to give birth, the four hundred ran up the mountain to attack the infant, with their sister leading the charge. But Huitzilopochtli, fully armed, was "born in an instant." Using his snakehead scepter, he decapitated the sister, and as her body rolled to the foot of the mountain it broke into pieces. Then, in a dizzying display of energy, he killed or routed all of her troops.

Fresh from this triumph over female authority, the hero became the protector of the wandering Mexica, serving as their spiritual war chief and leading them to the site of their future capital, Mexico City.

Quetzalcoatl himself, in one of his incarnations, was a heroic child not unlike Huitzilopochtli. "And from what they say about him," according to one of the old texts, "Quetzalcoatl was placed in his mother's belly when she swallowed a piece of jade."

In the usual story, however, the woman has a flesh-and-blood husband, who is murdered by the hero's jealous brothers (some say his uncles). To avenge his father's death, Quetzalcoatl sacrifices the assassins at the summit of a mountain, or pyramid. In one version, he rubs chili into their wounds to heighten their agony; in another, he orders drinking cups made from their skulls. This young hero, clearly, is a ruthless warrior.

The heroic child is also a familiar figure in southern Mexico and Guatemala, especially in the Mexican states of Oaxaca and Veracruz, where it is often said that the little boy was hatched from an egg. Such is the case with Homshuk, hero-god of the Popoluca; Kondoy of the Mixe; Fane Kansini of the Tequistlatec; and Tamacasti of the Veracruz Nahua.

Best known of the heroes born from eggs, however, is the so-called dwarf of Uxmal, whose story is recorded in Yucatec versions going back to the early nineteenth century. In a variant from the village of Chan Kom, more than a hundred miles east of the ruins of Uxmal, it is told that there was once a woman who found an egg, which she put into a gourd pot. Suddenly, three weeks later, she heard a baby crying.

The child grew rapidly and could walk and talk in just two months. Hearing that a king was collecting children to feed to his pet serpent, the boy allowed himself to be caught; and while in captivity, he killed the serpent with a sliver of glass. The king, seeking revenge, entered into a series of contests with the boy, culminating in an attempt to break his skull with palm nuts. Protected by a bronze hat, the child survived, then used the nuts to crush the king, becoming ruler in his place.

Other examples of the heroic-child motif would include the twin heroes of the Popol Vuh, whose contests with the lords of the underworld are in some instances the same as the trials endured by the hero born from an egg.

No doubt the colorful story is its own justification in the minds of many storytellers. But it may also have political or religious significance. For the Aztecs this magic child was a terror to all enemies and a spiritual force behind the building of the empire. Among the Tequistlatec it was believed that the heroic child—

Fane Kansini—had saved the tribe from the Zapotecs.

In Popoluca versions, the child's oppressor is the rain spirit, whose punishment, after he has been conquered, is to supply moisture for gardens. The hero himself, Homshuk, is the corn spirit, and the story as a whole becomes merged with The Man of Crops (myth ii).

It may be noticed that the twin heroes of myth xiv (The Childhood of Sun and Moon) are "heroic children" in the sense meant here. In fact, several variants specify that the boys are born from eggs and undergo rigorous trials beyond the conflict in which they outwit their old stepmother. The mythological significance is that they survive their adventures to become the sun and the moon.

In the case of the ancient Maya, the twins' adventures in the dead land are known not only from the Popol Vuh but from scenes on painted vases that have been found in tombs. One theory to account for these archaeological finds is that the twins' victory provided the deceased with a charm against the perils of the underworld.

The wise instructor

In contrast to the heroic child, who is born locally, the wise instructor is a traveler from an unspecified foreign land whose mission is cultural improvement. Europeans, especially Christian missionaries, have been eager to collect scraps of information on this subject, and it must be conceded that scraps are what we mostly have. In at least some cases, the story fragments reveal native attitudes about European colonization.

Among the Seri, it is told that a teacher called He Who Builds Fires came out of the west in a boat that moved by itself, without paddles. He was a tall, bearded "white man," who taught people to hunt, to use fire for cooking, and to make smoke signals. He also built houses and showed couples that they could live together as husband and wife; and since people often quarreled in those days, he taught them to live in peace. When his mission was

121

finished, he rose to the sky, where he still exists inside the sun.

Contradicting this account, some say that the man who built signal fires was God and that he came out of the south. Various tribes, seeing the smoke signals, came forth. But the Seri held back, and this is why Seri today are poor.

gl. Illustration #14 about here

Among the Aztecs, the instructor was Quetzalcoatl himself in yet another of his many guises. As a tall "white man" he came out of the east, had a beard said to have been either very long or very bushy, taught all the arts of civilization, and led a pure, priestly way of life. After serving for some years as ruler of the ancient Toltecs, or Chololtecs according to one version, he disappeared in the direction from which he had originally come.

The old Tzeltal hero called Votan is also said to have come from the east. He was a lawgiver and promoter of religious worship. In addition he taught hieroglyphic writing, the art of sculpture, and the cultivation of corn. When his work was complete, he entered the underworld through a cave.

Itzamná of the Yucatec was a similar teacher, responsible for hieroglyphic writing and the names of all geographical places. Upon his death, a city called Izamal was built over his grave.

Among other legendary instructors, one might mention Tioipitzintli (should be *Dios in piltzintli*, "God the son"), reported in the seventeenth century from the region of the Southern Tepehuan and the Huichol. Yet another is the so-called Ulikron (Orphan of the Virgin), whose story was chanted by Guaymí in the early twentieth century.

It is clear that such figures, though significant, are neither long-lasting nor deeply embedded in Middle American mythology. The Hidden Corn (myth ix) is the story that regularly accounts for the cultivation of maize, not the deeds of a teacher like Votan. Opossum Steals Fire is the Mexican myth that is being remembered and traded from tribe to tribe (myth iv), while the Seri story of He Who Builds Fires has little currency and a doubtful future.

Even Quetzalcoatl, if he is remembered at all, is no longer the wise instructor once celebrated by Aztec storytellers. The famous legend that bears his name is being kept alive in European, not Indian, languages.

The Flight of Quetzalcoatl

The expanded story of Quetzalcoatl, whether as heroic child or as peaceable instructor, makes much of his final departure, telling how he wandered from place to place until he reached the Gulf of Mexico. There he either died and was cremated or took to the water in a raft and disappeared. Often the hero's name is given as Topiltzin (Our Prince) or Ce Acatl (1 Reed), and usually he is said to have lived among the Toltecs.

Part of the legend, as it was circulated after the Conquest, was that Topiltzin Quetzalcoatl had promised to return in a year 1 Reed. And in fact, when the tall, white, bearded Cortés arrived in 1519, a year 1 Reed by the Aztec calendar was just coming around. For Aztecs, the legend explained the fate that had now caught up with them.

This is not to suggest that the story was entirely new. Many of the recorded versions tell how Topiltzin Quetzalcoatl had been driven from the Toltec capital by the sorcerer Tezcatlipoca. According to one account the sorcerer was none other than Tezcatlipoca the deity, also called Titlacahuan (We Are His Slaves), who had descended from the sky to make trouble for the Toltecs. Since Tezcatlipoca was a particular god of the Mexica, the leading tribe among the Aztecs, and since the Aztec empire was in reality a successor to the Toltec empire, the legend served to explain how the transition had come about.

In the most memorable of the versions that have been preserved, Quetzalcoatl is portrayed as a tragic victim of temptation. Lured into drunkenness by Tezcatlipoca, he becomes a figure of shame who has no choice but to renounce his throne and flee into exile.

The Flight of Christ

In twentieth-century Indian communities, the old heroes are often replaced by Christ, who, if one may judge from the stories, is less honored for his teachings than for his skill in avoiding persecution. Much of this material does not come from the Bible, as missionaries would no doubt prefer, but from medieval legends that must have arrived in Latin America with the earliest colonists.

gl. Illustration #15 about here

Indian versions of the life of Christ frequently include the courtship of the parents, Joseph and Mary, and the birth of the child in a filthy stable. The owners of comfortable houses who reject the holy family and the friendly cow who warms the child with her hot breath are among the usual characters.

The favorite episode, however, is a saga of the hero—often still a child—pursued by his enemies, whom he continually eludes. Before telling it, a Mazatec narrator may say, "Is there one among us who does not remember the story?"

As he runs from his pursuers, Christ meets birds and animals who either protect him or hinder him in his flight. The helpful creatures are rewarded; the unhelpful, punished.

Human bystanders play a role as well. Some are helpful, like the good man in the tale known as Christ and the Farmer. The man is just sowing his field as Christ goes by, but Christ causes the crops to mature in an instant. Then, when the pursuers arrive, the farmer says that the fugitive passed at sowing time. Seeing that the crops are now ready for harvest, the enemies assume they have lost the trail and turn off in a different direction. Thus, for a little while longer, Christ is saved from the inevitable crucifixion.

Occasionally this lore is grafted to a native tradition. For example, among the Tzotzil the hero Ohoroxtotil is said to have escaped his enemies by relying upon the ruse in Christ and the Farmer. The same is told of Piltonte (Little Boy), hero of the Nahua of Durango; also Homshuk, the Popoluca hero born from an egg.

In one of the Popoluca variants, the old woman who finds the egg cries out to her husband, "This is our laughter, our luck!" But, as we soon learn, the old couple's delight is in having found not a son but a source of food. When the boy has hatched and has grown plump, the two cannibals start talking about eating him. Overhearing their plans, the child kills the old man, then flees from the enraged old woman.

As he runs along, the boy—Homshuk—meets a farmer who has a banana patch. He says to the man, "If anyone passes by, you must say, 'The last time someone came this way was when I was planting my bananas, and now they are grown.'" So, when the old woman cames along, the good farmer deceives her, saying, "A man passed by when I was putting in these bananas, and now they have fruit." Thus the European legend, Christ and the Farmer, transferred to the native hero Homshuk.

Conversely, native lore may be borrowed to fill out the basically European story of Christ's life. In a Quiché version, after he has been caught by his pursuers, Christ's body becomes a source of food (myth ii: The Man of Crops). Just as he is being nailed to the cross, he turns around, exposing his back, and "from his back comes maize—white, yellow, and black—and beans and potatoes and all the other food plants."

In a telling reported from the Kanjobal, Christ becomes the hero of Sun and His Brothers (myth xv). Thus he manages to bring animals into the world, before meeting his pursuers and starting out on his flight.

Tricksters

It could be argued that Quetzalcoatl, Tezcatlipoca, the god Sibú, and even the Indian Christ are sometimes tricksters, who stoop to mischief in order to advance their own projects. But they are tricksters only in a very limited sense.

The classic trickster of native American mythology, whether of North or South America, is more than a deceiver. He is a fool, a dupe, and an imitator, incurably lecherous, greedy, vain, pretentious. Paradoxically, he brings order into the world, and often he is a gifted shaman. The most perfect examples are Coyote of the western United States, Raven of southern Alaska, and Fox of the Gran Chaco region of South America. The only Middle American hero who really belongs in this company is the Huichol trickster-god, Kauyumari, also known as Wolf.

In a typical series of Huichol stories, Kauyumari is duped repeatedly by Moon, who in the old days "measured the things of the world." Moon got Kauyumari to cut down a honey tree by flattering him, calling him "brother." But when the trickster took the honey in his hands, it turned into "stones and the black water that comes from hollow trees in the rainy season."

Moon gave Kauyumari a box of "food." But when he opened it, it was full of grasshoppers.

Moon encouraged Kauyumari to deliver a woman in childbirth. But under the trickster's care the woman gave birth to toads.

Another time, Kauyumari was shown a donkey, which, when beaten, would defecate silver coins. Kauyumari bought this donkey. But when he himself beat the animal and lifted its tail, expecting to see money, his face was covered with manure.

An extended cycle of creation stories, all fitted together in sequence, reveals the versatility of Kauyumari, who helps to establish the world as it is known today.

The series opens with a variant of Corn Woman's Marriage (myth x), in which the woman, though deeply offended by her mother-in-law, agrees to stay with her husband and bear him a son. When the son becomes ill, Kauyumari steps in and cures the boy, relying upon shamanic powers obtained from the sun.

When the boy grows up, he marries his own sister and their offspring populate the world.

But the people become too numerous. To save the earth from overcrowding, Sun orders Kauyumari to place teeth in the women's vaginas (a rare Middle American occurrence of the *vagina dentata* motif). As a result, all the men are mutilated, including Kauyumari. In the case of the trickster, however, his desire is so great that his missing organ promptly regenerates.

Disgusted with Sun's efforts, Nakawé, the earth mother, takes charge of the Creation and floods the world, saving only Kauyumari and a female dog (myth vi: The Flood Myth). The mating of the trickster and the dog gives rise to Hispanic Mexicans (not Indians).

Guided by Nakawé, a mystical deer-boy becomes the husband of one of a group of deer-women. Since these women have toothed vaginas, the goddess provides the trickster, Kauyumari, with a deer-horn covering and orders him to break the women's "teeth." After that, the boy mates with the women, and from this union the Huichol are born.

Later the trickster himself courts the deer-boy's wife, intending to marry her. But before the marriage can be consummated, the woman dies, and the trickster follows her to the dead land (myth xviii: The Dead Wife). Unable to bring her back alive, he performs the first Huichol funeral ceremonies, and in this way permanent death comes into the world.

Trickster stories elsewhere in Middle America are neither so varied nor so profound. This is not to say, however, that tricksters are little known. In fact, the antics of Coyote, Rabbit, and other animal characters are one of the staples of the region's folklore.

The Tar Baby is among the most popular of the tales. Rabbit, usually, is the clever trickster who persuades Coyote to take his place after he has been caught by a sticky little doll made of tar or wax.

In other stories, Rabbit breaks Coyote's teeth by dropping a hard fruit into his greedy mouth; burns him in a grass fire; stings him with a wasps' nest; or causes him to be drowned by diving for a "cheese" that is really the moon's reflection on the surface of the water.

These Rabbit-and-Coyote tales are of European origin and do not involve elements of world creation. Nevertheless they are highly valued, especially in southern Mexico and Guatemala. In the Tzotzil community of Chamula such stories are regarded as "ancient narrative"; and among the Kanjobal, storytellers may begin a humorous Rabbit yarn with the sober announcement: "A story of the ancestors, long ago."

The Devil's helpers

Heroes cannot be heroes unless they have adversaries. In some cases they borrow their opponents from the vast store of folk belief, elevating a common hobgoblin to the realm of myth and legend. In other cases the old hero-gods themselves become demons, proving the rule that yesterday's deities are today's spooks.

Middle American lore is rich in evil spirits. But it is well to keep in mind that the native supernaturals may combine both good and evil qualities, and one community's dread may be another's god.

Generally, the sharp distinction made today between helpful and harmful powers has a European origin. In fact, throughout the region the evil ones are likely to be called devils. Tarahumara say they are the Devil's helpers.

Names for these spirits are often borrowed from one village to the next, where they may be attached to somewhat different kinds of monsters. Accordingly, the much used term *tzitzimitl*—reappearing as *tzitzimat* or *sesimite* or *sinsirito*—may mean either an ogress or a gnome. The word itself is of unknown derivation. Other popular names are *sombrerón* (Spanish "big hat"), *duende* (Spanish "goblin"), and *chaneque* (Nahuatl "denizens"). The *chaneque*, also called *chaneques*, *chanekos*, or *chanekas*, may be either gnomes or temptresses.

The following brief catalog attempts to sort out the most prevalent types:

Giant. Oversized creatures, more or less human, are typically relegated to the ancient time and are said by some to have been the first race (as in variants of myth v: The Loss of the Ancients). In Popoluca lore, both male and female giants are still extant as forest-dwelling cannibals, believed to be so tall that there is no room anywhere for them to stretch out; they have to sleep sitting up.

gl. Illustration #16 about here

Gnome. This class of spirits merges with the rain dwarfs and the lords of the earth. Often operating in gangs, they are feared as kidnappers. Chinantec say that they are undersized and nude but have enormous ears with which they wrap themselves. A familiar variety known from Oaxaca to Panama has backward feet like the gnome called Kurupira in Brazil.

Man-eating bird. In variants of myth xiv (The Childhood of Sun and Moon) the boy heroes, once they have escaped their stepmother, slay a bloodthirsty bird that carries humans to its nest. Usually an eagle, the monster is known from northwest Mexico to Panama—and throughout the Americas. In a tale from the Nahua of Guerrero, the offending bird is the Plumed Serpent himself. Shot by a pair of local heroes, it makes a cross-country journey reminiscent of the flight of Quetzalcoatl.

Ogress. According to the Southern Tepehuan, the devouring woman has a huge ear that envelops her victims. Usually she is old, as in the story of the hero born from an egg, where she appears as the cruel stepmother. In Aztec lore, the skeletonlike *tzitzimitl* ogresses lived in the sky, waiting to pounce on humanity during solar eclipses or at the end of the world.

Sorcerer. The term *nagual* is widely used nowadays to mean an evildoer who changes himself into a animal or some other form— recalling the old Aztec word for sorcerer, *tlacatecolotl*, literally, "human owl." The god Tezcatlipoca plays this role in the legend of the flight of Quetzalcoatl; and naguals, or shape shifters, appear as villains in a variety of modern folktales.

129

Temptress. Irresistibly beautiful, the temptress lures men into an embrace of love, only to kill them or drive them insane. Her best-known incarnation is among the Yucatec, where she is called *xtabay* (pronounced shta-BYE). In Lacandon belief, male deities can enjoy the favors of the *xtabay* without mishap.

Water serpent. Intent on capturing humans, the great serpent inhabits pools and causes floods. Some specimens have horns.

Weeping Woman. Widely known as La Llorona ("the Weeping Woman"), this phantom of the night unnerves people with her eerie wailing. Some say she is crying for her lost children. Typically Mexican, she has been reported from the city of Los Angeles and as far south as Panama. Folklorists theorize that she represents a survival of myth iii (Why the Earth Eats the Dead). In Aztec lore, the hungry earth mother did indeed wail at night.

Belief in such spirits crosses the line between Indian and non-Indian culture. Throughout Middle America, people who have lost their Indian roots continue to report sightings of supernatural creatures, especially the temptress and the Weeping Woman. If the old myths were to die out, the spooks would remain alive.

4

Writing History

Two essential works

In large, complex societies, like those of ancient Mesoamerica, mythology is a prelude to the story of rulers and their nation's greatness. The complete account, which may take hours to recite (or read), becomes a history of the world as seen through the eyes of a particular people.

Unfortunately, the screen-fold books that have been preserved from pre-Conquest times do not record any of these extended histories. What remain of the old libraries are mostly almanacs, or ritual calendars—though Mixtec examples do preserve the stories of certain kings, embellished with details borrowed from myth.

The accompanying illustration is of the opening page from one of the Mixtec books, the Codex Nuttall, showing the ruler 8 Wind emerging from the earth at lower right, helped by a companion. The reader moves from this lower right-hand corner straight to the top of the page, then to the left and down to the bottom, and so on, the eye winding across the book from right to left in a snakelike fashion.

gl. Illustration #17 about here

Since there are no sentences, only pictures with symbols, the reader—or reciter—should know the story in advance and be able to use the long, streamerlike, opened book as a prompter. Here, then, we have the book but not the story (though modern scholars have had much success in deciphering its basic elements).

In other cases, we have the story but not the book; that is, the story was transcribed from screen-folds that became lost. Two famous examples are the Quiché Maya document called Popol Vuh and the Aztec Legend of the Suns. Both survive as texts that might once have been recited, and unlike the Codex Nuttall, these works are full-dress histories of the world, complete with accounts of the Creation and the deeds of gods.

The two texts, Popol Vuh and Legend of the Suns, were put into writing by native authors not long after the Conquest, using the European script. In their time they served to glorify the accomplishments of the Quiché Maya and the Mexica Aztecs. Today, four hundred years later, they are valued by the people of Mexico and Central America as cornerstones of their cultural heritage. For the study of Middle American mythology they are essential, if for no other reason than that so many people know them and refer to them. This is especially true of the Popol Vuh, which has often been spoken of as the single most important work of American Indian literature.

A review of the contents of these manuscripts will show that they have certain similarities. Both texts begin with mythic accounts of the world's origin, incorporating two stories that should by now be familiar, The Loss of the Ancients and The Hidden Corn. Both texts relate the deeds of gods or hero-gods in the time before dawn, and both make use of legends and cold facts to bring the story down to the time of the Spanish Conquest.

132

Popol Vuh

The anonymous author of the Quiché manuscript starts by saying, mysteriously, that the original *popol vuh* (council book) can no longer be seen. That work, we are told, described how earth and sky were divided into four parts by a primal pair called Mother and Father, also known as:

Former, Shaper
Majesty, Plumed Serpent
Green Plate Spirit [earth], Blue Bowl Spirit [sky]

And so forth. The text gives a dozen pairs of names for the primal mother-father, at least some of which are treated not as mere synonyms but as divine personalities in their own right.

The account is being written, however, "amid the preaching of God, in Christendom." And evidently this explains why the old myth of the earth's quartering is only mentioned, not told in full. Instead, we are given the story of Creation as set forth in the first chapter of the Christian Bible—although from a distinctly Indian point of view.

Rather than the lone spirit of God moving upon "the face of the waters," as in the biblical Creation, we have the primal couple hidden inside the waters and God, called Heart of Heaven, arriving in the sky. "It was good that you came," say the couple. The spirits converse, and by the power of their words earth appears out of the water and various plants and creatures are made. There is no sun, however. As yet the only light is a glow that comes from the spirit powers within the water.

The native author now leaves the Bible behind—at least for the most part—and slips into a narrative framework dictated by The Loss of the Ancients (myth v).

Thinking to perfect their work, the gods create mammals and birds and order them to recite prayers. But the creatures only "hissed and screamed and cackled." Because they failed to worship, they were banished to the wilderness to be hunted as game. Thus the loss of the first race of ancients.

Next the spirits made a human body out of clay. But it was soft and limp, and "as soon as it spoke, it made no sense." Disgusted, the gods destroyed it.

In a third attempt, the spirits fashioned people out of wood. These looked and acted like humans and were able to populate the earth. But there was "nothing in their minds." They did not know how to worship the gods. To get rid of them, Heart of Heaven sent a flood; jaguars came and tore the people's flesh; and even their utensils revolted against them and struck them down. Those that survived went into the forest to become monkeys.

The fourth and final attempt to create humans now waits to be told. But it will mark the end of the myth age. Therefore, while the world is still in darkness, the narrator takes the opportunity to relate two major exploits of the twin hero-gods Hunahpu and Xbalanque (pronounced shbalan-KAY), which will ultimately account for the origin of the sun. In the first of these adventures, the twins defeat a family of tricksters who falsely claim to be gods. In the second, they descend to the underworld and defeat the lords of death.

The trickster family consists of a bright-faced father, who calls himself the sun, and his two offspring, Cabracan, who boasts of shaking the earth, and Zipacna, who claims to be the earth maker. True to the nature of tricksters, they love to eat, and it is this that proves their undoing. The hero-gods simply lure them into one trap or another, always baited with food.

Perhaps Zipacna is the most memorable of the trio. One of his well-known stunts is to wriggle out of a pitfall that has been prepared for him by a gang of adversaries: they wait to hear his death scream, then run off congratulating themselves, while Zipacna, whose cry has been just an act, emerges from the pit unhurt. (Today the deeds of the trickster Zipacna are still told by the Achi of western Guatemala.) The second and more serious of the twin heroes' adventures is their descent to the underworld.

It is a complicated story, told skillfully by the Popol Vuh author, who weaves together a mass of mythic material in the manner of a modern novelist, using flashbacks and subplots.

The sequence begins with a flashback to the time of the heroes' father, who, with *his* brother, had gone to the underworld to play ball with the death lords and had been killed. In the form of a skull, the dead ballplayer hangs from a tree, catches the attention of an underworld maiden, and, by spitting into the palm of her hand, impregnates her.

Aware of her condition, the maiden seeks shelter in the house of an old grandmother who lives on the earth's surface. Soon the twin heroes are born. But, as the rapidly growing boys soon discover, they must contend with two other grandsons, whom the old woman favors. To rid themselves of their abusive rivals, the heroes send them up a stretching tree, where, happily, they are transformed into monkeys (a variant of myth xv: Sun and His Brothers).

Now, against the old woman's wishes, Hunahpu and Xbalanque descend to the underworld to play ball with the death lords, just as their father had done. Before the game can begin, however, the lords subject the two boys to a series of trials, including imprisonment in a house of darkness, a house of knives, a house of jaguars, and a house of bats. Through cleverness the heroes survive these tests and prevail in the ball game as well.

Then, to tempt the lords of death, the heroes show how they can kill a man and bring him back to life. Fascinated, the lords beg to be given the same treatment. The heroes glady comply, but only halfway. The death lords are slain and not revived. Victorious, Hunahpu and his brother now rise to the sky, becoming the sun and the moon.

Or eventually they do. As we will soon be reminded, the world's first dawn has not yet appeared.

At this point the creator-spirits reenter, wondering if they can at last make humans. As they gather their thoughts, four animals bring corn, called "food," from the inside of a mountain (myth ix: The Hidden Corn). "And these are the animals who brought

135

the food: fox, coyote, parrot, crow." Adding water to the corn, the gods make the flesh of four male ancestors, who are then provided with four wives.

gl. Illustration #18 about here

The people begin to increase. Since they are cold, the god Tohil (Torch Mirror) drills fire. But he gives it to the people only if they promise him human victims, who are to be sacrificed by having their hearts ripped out. After the agreement has been made, the people assemble on a mountain to watch for the first dawn.

As the sun comes up, Tohil and other gods are turned to stone, becoming idols. Animals of the ancient time, especially jaguars and other predators, are also changed to stone at the first sunrise. "Perhaps we would not be living today," writes the author, "if these [dangerous] first animals had not been turned to stone by the sun."

Thereafter war is instituted for the purpose of capturing live victims for sacrifice to the gods. As the Quiché nation grows strong, the ancestors, who had been made from corn, die and are replaced by succeeding generations.

In the twelfth generation the Spaniards arrive, conquering the Quiché and putting their rulers to death (in the year 1524). Two more generations of native rulers—puppet rulers under Spanish authority—are named, bringing the Quiché history down to the 1550s, the decade in which the Popol Vuh was written.

Legend of the Suns

Like the Popol Vuh, the Aztec Legend of the Suns is a world history built on the idea of repeated creations. Such events, presumably, take place during an indefinite myth time. Yet here the native author has a clear sense of when it all began. As he tells us in his opening statement, the world is "2513 years old today,

May 22, 1558" — a computation both more precise and less cautious than the estimate given out by Christian missionaries, who believed that five thousand years had elapsed between the Creation and the birth of Christ.

In general, the Legend of the Suns is free of European influence, and even the notion of calculating the world's age may date from before the Conquest. Aztecs are known to have been exquisitely conscious of numbers, and in any case the figures are based on the Aztec, not the Christian, calendar.

The first age, or "sun," we are told, lasted 676 years, which makes 13 cycles of 52 years each (the natural unit, since the Aztec calendar repeats itself after a 52-year "round"). At the end of this time the sun was destroyed, and the people who had lived under it were eaten by jaguars.

The second sun had a shorter life. After 364 years (or 7 rounds), it was simply blown away by the wind, while the people on earth were swept off and changed into monkeys.

A third sun arose, but it had been in the sky for just 6 calendar rounds when it was burned in a rain of fire. The fire also scorched the earthlings, who were changed into turkeys.

The fourth sun, like the first, lasted 13 rounds. But this time the end came in a flood, and the ancient people were drowned and changed into fish.

It should perhaps be emphasized that these repeated variants of myth v (The Loss of the Ancients), even if a flood is included, are not the same as the Mesoamerican Flood Myth (myth vi). That important story has a plot all its own. To incorporate it, the careful author now pauses to explain in greater detail what happened at the end of the fourth sun.

It seems that the god Tezcatlipoca appeared to a couple called Tata and Nene, warning them of the flood and instructing them to save themselves in a hollowed out log. They are to take corn with them (to be planted after the flood?); but when the flood is over, the disobedient couple have eaten all the kernels and must catch fish to feed themselves.

To roast the fish, they build a fire. But the gods, smelling the smoke, are annoyed, and Tezcatlipoca himself comes down from the sky to mete out the punishment: "he cut off their heads and stuck them on their rumps, and that way they were turned into dogs."

And now—just as in the Popol Vuh—the author postpones the final creation in order to hand down the various myths that must be included while the "darkness" prevails.

First, Tezcatlipoca (Smoking Mirror) drills fire. Then the spirits begin asking each other, "Who will there be? Sky has been established, Earth has been established. Spirits, who will there be?" As in the Popol Vuh, the gods take the mystic form of a couple, multiplied several times to form a council of spirits. They are called:

Skirt of Stars, Star Shine

Quetzalcoatl [Plumed Serpent], Titlacahuan [another name for Tezcatlipoca]

—and various other pairs of names. The result of their conference is that Quetzalcoatl is sent to the underworld to get the bones of the ancients, from which a new race will be born.

As Quetzalcoatl approaches the dead land lord, he calls out, "I've come for the precious bones that you are keeping. I've come to get them." Then the dead land lord asks, "To do what, Quetzalcoatl?" And he explains, "It's because the spirits are sad, [asking,] 'Who will there be on earth?'" The dead land lord replies, "Very well, [take them.]"

But despite this word of consent, he tries three times to prevent the bones from being taken. First he gives Quetzalcoatl a solid horn and insists that he play it. With the aid of animal helpers, Quetzalcoatl outwits him, summoning worms who hollow it out, then bees who roar inside it, making it play.

Next the lord tells his servants to forbid Quetzalcoatl from removing the bones. But Quetzalcoatl tricks them by promising to obey their command while hurriedly covering the bones in a wrapper and starting off with them.

Seeing that he has been deceived, the lord has his servants dig a pit. As Quetzalcoatl stumbles into the trap, the bones spill; and the quail—the birds of the underworld—bite into them and nibble them.

But even though the bones have been nibbled and thus "ruined" (meaning that humans will not be immortal?), Quetzalcoatl picks them up again and carries them to the sky. There they are ground to a powder and placed in a bowl by the goddess Cihuacoatl (Snake Woman). Then all the other gods shed blood into the bowl, saying, "Humans have been born."

Again the spirits confer, asking each other, "Spirits, what will they eat?"

By way of an answer, Quetzalcoatl changes himself into an ant, brings corn kernels out of Food Mountain (myth ix: The Hidden Corn), and carries these kernels to the council of spirits. "Then the spirits chew them and put them on our lips. That's how we grew strong."

After thunder has split open Food Mountain, releasing all the different kinds of corn and other foods, the gods assemble once again, this time at the place called Teotihuacán. Here they select a spirit called Nanahuatl, telling him, "You are the one who must keep the sky and the earth."

When the "spirit oven" at Teotihuacán has been lit, Nanahuatl leaps into the flames and becomes the sun; a second spirit, who follows him, just lands in the ashes, becoming the much paler moon (myth xii: The Sun and the Fire).

The new sun now appears in the east. Yet it does not move into its course. "Why doesn't he move?" ask the gods. A falcon is sent to query him. "Why?" replies the sun. "Because I am asking for their blood, their color, their precious substance."

At first angry, the gods relent and allow themselves to be sacrificed. "And there in Teotihuacán they all died a sacrificial death. So then the sun went in the sky. And then goes the moon, who had fallen only in the ashes. And when he got to the edge of the sky, Papaztac [one of the 400 "rabbits," or wine gods] came and broke his face with a rabbit pot [which explains the origin of the moon's spots—that is, the 'rabbit' in the moon]."

The manuscript implies that this fifth sun, the sun named Nanahuatl, was created shortly after the destruction of the fourth sun, which would bring the story up to approximately the 2028th year after the world's beginning. Subtracting that figure from 2513 years, the world's age in A.D. 1558 (as told in the opening paragraph of the manuscript), we now find ourselves in the eleventh century A.D.—about the right time for the appearance of the Mexica Aztecs and the decline of their predecessors, the Toltecs.

In an unusual variant of myth i (The Emergence of Ancestors), the author explains that the five original Mexica were born in a cave called Chicomoztoc (seven cave place), where they were suckled by the spirit Mecitli, who "is Earth." As yet, however, these ancestral Mexica are known as the five Mixcoa.

An unsuccessful tribe called the 400 Mixcoa are also born at this time and are commanded by the sun himself to "give the sun a drink." Neglecting their duty, the foolish 400 fall prey to the warlike five, who sacrifice the 400, thus fulfilling the sun's command.

Two unlucky stragglers, Xiuhnel and Mimich, escape the bloodletting only to be overwhelmed by a pair of murderous deer women (Xiuhnel is eaten alive, Mimich is reduced to tears). Then a band of fire spirits, evidently on behalf of the valiant five, steps forward, and the deer women are mystically transformed by fire into a war bundle, which becomes Mixcoatl's charm in battle.

Mixcoatl goes on to defeat an army of warrior women, one of whom becomes his consort. Together they produce the heroic child 1 Reed. But by the time 1 Reed is born, Mixcoatl has been murdered by three additional stragglers from the tribe of the 400. 1 Reed hunts down these odious "uncles" and sacrifices them at the summit of a pyramid dedicated to his father. After that, he proceeds eastward, making conquests at every stop, until he reaches the seashore, where he dies and is cremated.

The story of the hero 1 Reed is a variant of the legend of the flight of Quetzalcoatl, ousted ruler of the Toltecs. But the author here uses it to illustrate the custom of human sacrifice rather than to make a statement about the fall of Tula.

Without further reference to 1 Reed, the account continues with a series of plagues and omens that beset the Toltecs, including a prophecy by the rain gods to the effect that the Mexica will inherit their power. We next find the Mexica, presumably the descendants of the original five that had been suckled by Mecitli, heading southward from Aztlan, their ancestral home. (Though the manuscript does not make the connection, Aztlan in other sources is identified with the "seven cave place" of the emergence.)

Entering the Valley of Mexico, the wandering Mexica suffer hardships, manage with difficulty to found their capital, and begin to build what will become the Aztec empire. The Mexica rulers, with lists of their conquests, are named down to Montezuma the Elder (ruled A.D. 1440–1468).

Here the manuscript breaks off, its final page or pages having been lost over the course of the centuries. But from other Aztec sources the rest of the story is easily supplied: after Montezuma the Elder, Mexico was ruled by Axayacatl, who was succeeded by Tizoc, then Ahuitzotl, then Montezuma the Younger, who was on the throne—who held the "mat and seat"—in 1519, when the Spaniards arrived. Presumably the final page of the manuscript continued down to the puppet ruler Cecepatic, whose term of office had four more years to go when the Legend of the Suns was reduced to writing in the spring of 1558. (These last few facts are not in dispute; they are attested by Sahagún and other sixteenth-century authors, both Hispanic and Indian).

Like the Popol Vuh, the Legend of the Suns departs from the far shores of myth and after a long voyage comes to port within the realm of history.

But where did the author cross the line? Among scholars today, there are some who believe that Aztlan, the place of emergence, is a real location; others are doubtful. Some see shreds of fact in the adventures of the Mixcoa, while for others the safe ground of history is not approached until about the time of Montezuma the Elder.

As the debate continues, the texts from beginning to end are lovingly preserved, reexamined, and republished. In effect the old authors, by weaving tradition into a historical fabric, have smuggled their ancient mythologies into the future.

This is because history, with its true-to-life dates, places, and persons, is commonly accepted in the modern world and will continue to reign unchallenged, even if we do not lose our fascination with the dreamlike inner truths revealed by myth. Indeed, myth has not lost its power. Yet its value for modern people is enhanced if it can be comfortably embedded in history or if, in itself, it can give the illusion of history. Myth that falls into this privileged category, and only such myth, can be used today for public as well as private purposes. This is the myth that can create that special sense of an illustrious past which helps to build modern nations.

5

Myths and Nationalism

An emerging heritage

Organized in the 1500s as the colony called New Spain, Middle America won its independence in 1821 and became, briefly, the "Mexican Empire."

Two years later, Central America broke off from what would henceforth be called Mexico, and by 1839 the breakaway region had split into the republics of Guatemala, Honduras, El Salvador, Nicaragua, and Costa Rica. (Panama, originally grouped with Spain's South American colonies, separated from Colombia in 1903; and Belize, a special case, is a part of Guatemala taken over by Great Britain.)

Such names and dates fit comfortably into the history of Europe in America. But what they fail to reveal is that the citizens of Mexico and its neighbor republics are mostly Indian people and people who have at least some Indian ancestry. This is a truth that has claimed increasing attention in the years since independence, as elected, or designated, governments struggle to accommodate a tradition of Spanish rule to the needs of a

143

very American population.

Even today there is a side to Mexico, its Spanish side, that keeps its Indian background concealed. There is another side, however, that celebrates Indianness as an essential ingredient in Mexico's national character. Many Mexicans have come to feel that Indian art, architecture, history, and even mythology contribute to the nation's culture and help to define Mexico in relation to the other countries of the world.

Similar feelings may be detected in Central America, though on a smaller scale and with variations determined by the history of each nation.

To a degree the native mythology of Middle America has escaped its Indian background and entered the Spanish-speaking mainstream. At the same time, mythology continues to be nourished in Indian communities, often at cross purposes with the goals of central governments in Mexico City, Guatemala City, and other Middle American capitals—as we shall see.

Our Lady of Guadalupe

During the war of Mexican independence, which lasted from 1810 to 1821, patriots rallied to an image of Christ's mother that was felt to be uniquely Mexican. In the name of religion and for the sake of the homeland, all soldiers were required to wear her picture.

Known as Our Lady of Guadalupe, the holy woman was believed to have appeared on Mexican soil just ten years after the Conquest of 1521, asking that a church be built in her honor. The site she chose was the little hill of Tepeyacac, now called Villa Guadalupe or Villa Madero, about four miles north of the center of Mexico City.

Tepeyacac was actually the site of an old shrine of the goddess Tonantzin (Our Mother), one of several Aztec deities representing female power. The earth mother, the one who wailed at

144

night and demanded the blood of human victims, was sometimes called Tonantzin. But the Tonantzin of Tepeyacac was Teteo Innan (Mother of the Gods), the special patroness of midwives and healers.

Prior to the Conquest, Aztec pilgrims had traveled to the shrine of Tonantzin from all parts of the Valley of Mexico, presumably in search of cures. When Spaniards replaced her temple with a church dedicated to the Virgin of Guadalupe (whose cult was already long established in Spain), Aztecs continued to come to Tepeyacac for the same purpose as before.

Cures were now attributed to the Virgin. But native people—as they do to this day—still called her Tonantzin.

Worshipped by Spaniards and Indians alike, the Mexican Virgin gained in popularity through the 1500s and early 1600s. Finally, in 1649, the priest in charge of the church at Tepeyacac, a certain Luis Lasso de la Vega, published a little story that had the effect of severing Our Lady of Guadalupe from her Spanish roots.

gl. Illustration #19 about here

It was Lasso's account that established 1531 as the date of the Lady's appearance in Mexico. As Lasso explains, the Virgin appeared to a poor Indian named Juan Diego in December of that year, telling him to ask the bishop to build a church on the spot where she was standing.

Predictably, the bishop would not listen to a poor Indian. Again the Lady appealed to Juan Diego, and again the bishop turned him away. The third time, she gave him fresh roses to take to the bishop as a sign.

Seeing the flowers, which could not have bloomed naturally in December, the bishop's heart was softened. And then, when the roses had been handed over, a portrait of the Lady miraculously appeared on Juan Diego's cloak. Falling to his knees, the bishop gave orders for a church to be built at Tepeyacac.

In a preface to his published account, dedicated to the Virgin herself, Lasso says, "I have written your miracle in the Nahuatl language . . . please accept it in my humble words." Despite this admission of authorship, many people believe that Lasso's story is a legend obtained from Indian informants. Others, perhaps a majority, consider it factual, not a legend. Still others, including Indians, pay it little attention.

Although Indian people appreciate "Guadalupe" as a worker of cures and as a protector of Indian interests, Lasso's story did not slip into oral tradition. Folktale collections do not include variants of it. (On the other hand, the story's popularity cannot be denied, and it has evidently inspired local religious movements—as in Michoacán State, where in 1973 an image of the Virgin of the Rosary was said to have miraculously appeared on a piece of cloth.)

But even Spanish-speaking Mexicans who, out of healthy skepticism, distance themselves from the legend agree that Our Lady of Guadalupe, with her strong appeal to religious faith and patriotism, is a force for national unity. For many, believers and nonbelievers alike, Tonantzin-Guadalupe embodies the essence of Mexico.

The eagle and the serpent

The image of the Virgin, even if it could be reliably traced to 1531, is not Mexico's oldest national symbol. That distinction belongs to the emblem of the city of Mexico, traceable to pre-Columbian times and adapted by Spanish colonists for their own use in the 1500s. Two hundred years after the Conquest it became the official emblem of the Mexican republic.

Over the centuries the design has varied, showing an eagle perched on a prickly pear cactus, sometimes with a smaller bird held in its claws, or, as today, with a serpent in its beak.

According to Aztec legend, the wandering Mexica left Aztlan, their place of emergence, under the guidance of the god Huitzilopochtli. As they traveled along, the deity advised them to watch for an eagle perched on a prickly pear. This would be their sign. When at last they saw it, they founded their new capital on that spot, calling it Tenochtitlan (place of the rock tuna, a species of prickly pear, or tuna, that grows among rocks). Tenochtitlan was also called Mexico, and it was under this name that the city entered the colonial era and, subsequently, the era of independence.

Revolution and its symbols

The war of Mexican independence, though it began as a social revolution and thereby won Indian support, ended as a transfer of power from Spaniards who had been born in Spain to Spaniards who had been born in New Spain. Most people of Indian ancestry continued to work for wealthy landowners and to endure a legal system that did not protect their interests.

Some reforms were enacted during the 1800s, especially in the time of Benito Juárez, the Zapotec Indian who served as President of Mexico through most of the third quarter of the century. More meaningful reforms waited until the Mexican Revolution of 1910–1917, which, if it did not fully live up to its promise, ushered in a new era of pride and hope.

As of the late 1980s Central America had not been able to duplicate the Mexican achievement, or had done so only fitfully. But revolutionary movements were active in Guatemala and El Salvador, and a revolutionary regime in Nicaragua—the so-called Sandinista government—had been in power since 1979.

The new concept of nationhood required a set of symbols that could stand apart from the legacy of tyranny associated with Europe and colonialism. Mexico chose to emphasize its Aztec heritage, and revolutionaries in Central America, similarly, have identified with Aztec and Maya themes.

Remembering the myth of Quetzalcoatl and the dead-land bones (as told in the Legend of the Suns), the Nicaraguan poet Ernesto Cardenal wrote the following lines when the Nicaraguan revolution was still a distant dream:

147

If there isn't but dust in the pot
it is because mother Snake Woman is grinding me as on a grindstone
and my blossoming bones will revive!
Quetzalcoatl will take me from the dead land.

Another well-known Nicaraguan poet, Pablo Antonio Cuadra, writing on the eve of the revolution, recalled the death of one of the prominent guerrilla fighters, comparing him to the twin heroes of the Popol Vuh:

A hero struggled against the lords of the
*   House of Bats,*
against the lords of the House of Darkness.

Drawing upon a different myth, also from the Popol Vuh, the Salvadoran novelist Manlio Argueta compares the loss of the ancients (who became monkeys at the close of the third creation) to the depraved condition of those who support a repressive military regime. "Today," he writes, scornfully, "they are monkeys, apes, gorillas."

In Latin America, unlike the United States, poets enjoy considerable influence. But even if they use Aztec and Maya themes, they do not necessarily speak for modern Indians living in Indian communities. The inclusion of poets in the highest circles of the Sandinista government has not spared Nicaragua from charges of persecuting its own Indian population, the Mískito and the Sumu of the Caribbean coast.

Emphasizing the mysterious

With their ferocious deities demanding human blood, Aztecs intentionally terrified other Indian nations. This was one means of facilitating conquest. Today, preserved in myths and monumental artworks, the Aztec strategy has not lost its power to inspire awe. For some observers, generally from outside Mexico,

148

fascination gives way to distaste and even disapproval.

But occasional squeamishness cannot prevent modern Mexico from displaying the great calendar stone, also called sun stone, with its central figure of the earth deity, tongue protruding and teeth bared (illustrated in Part Three, chapter 2, above).

Mexico is proud of its Day of the Dead, an annual festival that can be traced to the Aztec *miccailhuitl* (dead feast or dead day); and it takes pleasure in its profusion of art objects, craft items, even candies and children's toys, that feature human skulls.

The fearful Weeping Woman who still haunts the countryside—an echo of the hungry earth mother—has been celebrated in Mexican art, literature, and film.

With this kind of lore in mind, the Mexican poet and essayist Octavio Paz has written, "For Mexicans, death sees and touches itself: it is the body emptied of the soul, the pile of bones that somehow, as in the Aztec poem, must bloom again." What Paz refers to as the "poem" is the myth of Quetzalcoatl's dead-land bones that has been mentioned more than once in this book (and was used by the poet Cardenal, as noted).

The open acceptance of death is part of what Paz calls the "Indian element" in Mexican culture. "In the United States," he writes, "the Indian element does not appear. This, in my opinion, is the major difference between our two countries."

gl. Illustration #20 about here

With less reserve than Paz, the writer Aurelio Ballados, a resident of Veracruz State, has expressed a similar attitude in his defiant poem *Patria morena* ("Dark Land," literally "Dark-complexioned Homeland"), published in 1981:

> *Dark land! With fervor I call your name,*
> *bells ringing in my throat. . . ..*
>
> *I believe in the storied crimson of your myths.*
> *I reverence your thousand idolatries.*

I love the abyss of your mythologies.
The blood of your rituals is my communion.
I believe in your sun stones, your infallible
calendars a thousand times millenarian. . . . .

Mexico! The forbidden pain is yours,
for you are a land of nobility and art. . . .

But this line of inquiry can be carried too far.

In search of the humane

However artistic the ancient lore may have been, most modern Mexicans do not see themselves as the descendants of bloodletting ritualists. While not denying the grandeur of even the most mysterious of the old traditions, people today take particular comfort in the sixteenth-century legend of Quetzalcoatl the wise instructor, especially in those variants that portray him as the enemy of human sacrifice.

According to one of the old texts, "Sorcerers tried to ridicule Quetzalcoatl into making the human payment, into taking human lives. But he always refused. He did not consent, because he greatly loved his subjects, who were Toltecs. Snakes, birds, and butterflies that he killed are what his sacrifices always were."

An even gentler variant has it that his offerings to the gods were "nothing but bread and flowers."

An appreciation of this tradition is evident in the series of murals painted by the Mexican artist José Clemente Orozco, contrasting the white-robed Toltec, Quetzalcoatl, with the grim warriors of the Mexica Aztecs. These pictures, at Dartmouth College, are among several important works painted in the United States by Mexican mural artists in the 1930s.

Another reassuring tradition is that of the Texcocan king Nezahualcoyotl, whose realm lay just to the east of the Mexica. Actually, the sixteenth-century records pertaining to Nezahualcoyotl are a mixture of history and legend adapted to the myth of the heroic child—a little boy miraculously reborn as a warrior who outwits a cruel tyrant and thereby avenges the death of his father. But in the seventeenth century, thanks to the writings of the Mexican historian Fernando de Alva Ixtlilxóchitl, this tradition was remade.

Ixtlilxóchitl himself, legitimately, it seems, claimed descent from Nezahualcoyotl, who in turn was now said to have been a descendant of Quetzalcoatl. According to the newly revealed information, Nezahualcoyotl had been a great "poet" and "philosopher," who had worshipped a single god and had known that the righteous go to heaven and the wicked suffer in hell. Moreover, like Quetzalcoatl, Nezahualcoyotl had objected to human sacrifice.

In a guerrilla poem of the 1960s, scorning the "Nazi" Mexica, Ernesto Cardenal portrays the poet-king Nezahualcoyotl in terms that would be congenial to many:

> He overthrew tyrants and military juntas.
>> As for human sacrifices, no. He
>> did not agree.
>>> That was not his religion.
> Only songs make us great, not war.

As Cardenal's verses imply, there are two sides to Nezahualcoyotl: the warlike (when necessary) and the humane (which makes us "great").

A new Aztlan

Mexican nationalism is felt not only in Middle America but in the southwestern United States, where Mexicans in small numbers have lived for three hundred years and where many more have settled in recent decades.

For Mexicans in the United States, or Chicanos as many prefer to be called, the Southwest is a region to which they naturally belong. As expressed by the Chicano poet Ricardo Sánchez:

my lands were
new mexico, colorado,
california, arizona, texas,
and many other pathways . . .

These lands were in fact taken by force from Mexico by the United States during the period 1836–48. In the 1960s, as their numbers grew, Chicanos started referring to the lost region as Aztlan, recalling the legend of the wandering Mexica. Some have even called themselves Aztecs, or *aztecas*.

gl. Illustration #21 about here

Seeking to build unity in the face of discrimination, Chicanos began borrowing the symbols of Mexican nationalism, including Our Lady of Guadalupe, the god-man Quetzalcoatl, and the eagle and the serpent. The fast-developing Chicano literary and artistic movement has drawn upon feelings of rage, despair, defiance—and hope, as expressed by the writer Juan Felipe Herrera in his poem "Quetzalcoatl":

quetzalcoatl
no sorrow
shining
quetzalcoatl
plumed heart
of struggle
happy
working
transforming
dying constellations . . .
conscious heart
suffering
rejoicing

152

in the work
in the plumed heart struggle
turning earth over
milpa of la raza
la raza-*milpa*
glowing heart fifth sun . . .
a new cycle . . .
plumed heart struggle
deserving
lord-lady
life giver
ever present ever near.

Although the term *la raza* (the race), meaning the Chicano people, has been left untranslated, this English version of Herrera's poem cannot show, unfortunately, that the original lines were composed in a mixture of Spanish, English, and Nahuatl, reflecting the fusion of three cultures.

Native voices

The question of who is an Indian is a difficult one. Many Chicanos, for example, identify themselves as Indians on the basis of ethnic heritage. But if the label is reserved for people who continue to speak Indian languages and live in Indian communities, most Mexicans and Chicanos would be excluded. For those who remain—the native people—it would have to be granted that nationalism, regardless of the Aztec and Maya symbolism that goes with it, is not a welcome idea.

Native communities in Mexico and Central America have their own political agendas, which call for communal ownership of the land and home rule. Most do not seek to become separate states, at least not today. But neither do they wish to be overwhelmed by outsiders.

Over the years, mythology has helped these communities

153

maintain their separateness, giving them a source of spiritual power that cannot be taken away. Not only have the people preserved basic myths from pre-Columbian times, but in many instances they have developed new mythologies, especially in times of crisis. The new lore centers around two principal themes, the Indian Christ or Virgin and the Indian King.

The first of these, though essentially Christian, has the effect of reinforcing Indian values, as a few well-known cases will show:

The Lord of Calvary. Among the Nahua of southern Puebla State it is told that a certain image of Christ, located on a hill now called Calvary (Calvario), unnailed himself from the cross and turned brown to match the color of his Indian worshippers. As the news spread, the shrine at Calvario began to attract crowds of pilgrims.

The crucified Christ of Chamula. In the year 1867, in the Tzotzil community of Chamula, a young woman came forward with three stones that she said had fallen from the sky. Clay figurines were added to the stones, and it was claimed that the young woman had given birth to them and was herself the mother of God. The following year, under the direction of the native leader Pedro Díaz Cuzcat, a ten-year-old Tzotzil boy was nailed to a cross in order to provide native people with a Christ of their own. Alarmed, Mexican authorities intervened, provoking the so-called Cuzcat Rebellion, which was not put down until 1870.

The Virgin of Cerro Amarillo. In 1956 a young woman of the Southern Tepehuan reported seeing the Virgin of Guadalupe at a place called Cerro Amarillo (Yellow Hill). The Virgin had spoken to her, she said, requesting that a chapel be built in her honor and advising that the people continue the *mitotes*, or native dances. In addition, they were to stop wearing Mexican clothes. The chapel was built, and the community began to strengthen its Indian customs.

The Virgin of the Guaymí. In 1962, among the Guaymí of western Panama, a young woman received a message from the Virgin and her "husband," Jesus, who emerged from the depths of a river to tell her that the Guaymí must avoid all contact with Latin civilization. Thereafter known as Mama Chi, the young woman instructed the people to shun Latins, to take their children out of school, and to throw away their national identification cards.

Notice that the withdrawal from national culture is the recurring theme through all these episodes.

More threatening to non-Indians than the modified Christian cults are the legends of Indian kings, which recall the trauma of the Conquest and hold out the promise of a return to political, not just spiritual, power. This kind of lore has been reported from a vast territory, ranging from the Pueblos of New Mexico, where the return of Montezuma was once predicted, all the way to the Central Andes, where Indian people still await the Inca king, called Inkarrí. A few twentieth-century examples from Middle America will show that the concept is still alive in the central region as well:

The Chatino king. Chatin, king of the Chatino tribe, is the one who gave the people their religious customs—in the days before there were factory-made clothes. When the Spaniards came, they took Chatin to Mexico City and removed his crown. He has not been able to return.

Montezuma of the Popoluca. The Popoluca say that before Montezuma came to them, the people went naked. He showed them how to dress in clothes. He was a great fighter. But when "someone" stole his "wife," he went off to Mexico City, where he was "poisoned." (The "someone" is possibly Cortés, who took the *daughter* of Montezuma as his mistress and hanged her husband, the Mexica king Cuauhtemoc, who was indeed a "great fighter.")

Cuasrán. The Indians of Costa Rica tell of Cuasrán, also called Father Volcano, who fled the Spaniards at the time of the Conquest and still lives surrounded by riches in pre-Columbian style. From time to time he carries people off with him to share his life inside the volcano.

The Maya King. Yucatec say that the king of the Maya is hiding, perhaps underground at Chichén Itzá. Someday he will return with "our brothers in work," the ancients who built the great

155

cities of Yucatan.

Tecun Uman. In 1523, when the Spaniards came to conquer the Quiché of Guatemala, the war chief Tecun Uman went out to meet them. The Spaniards killed Tecun, but according to legend his *nagual*, or alter ego, which was the quetzal bird, lived on and continued fighting the invaders. In the 1980s, as the Quiché attempted to defend themselves against the Guatemalan army, people updated the story, saying that Tecun had returned, bringing with him two million warriors to aid the Indian cause.

Lore of this type, though current, is not entirely new. Efforts to revive Indian leaders may be traced to the sixteenth century, when Aztec ritualists defied the Spaniards by summoning old kings from the region of the dead. In songs accompanied by drumming and dancing, the performers called out to Montezuma, Nezahualcoyotl, and other great figures, inviting them to return with their warriors. After witnessing such rituals, an envoy from the royal court of Spain wrote, "In these [songs] they speak of conspiracy against ourselves."

If the time is ripe, the new lore may develop hand in hand with armed resistance. Or, as in the Aztec case, it may be used as a substitute when military action fails or is no longer an option.

As the twentieth century draws to a close, local autonomy can at least be bargained for, as in Nicaragua, or publicly demanded, as by the recent Indian congresses held in Mexico. These meetings have called for increased landholdings, local management of natural resources, Indian control of the Mexican bureau of Indian affairs, and the expulsion of the Summer Institute of Linguistics.

Armed conflict, though it has erupted in Guatemala, no longer appears to be a factor in Mexico, though the Mexican government was suppressing would-be rebellions as recently as the 1970s. During the nineteenth century, as is well known, there were violent clashes in Chiapas, in Yucatan, and, notably, in northwest Mexico among the Yaqui.

Yaqui troops held out against Mexican occupation of their territory until the 1890s. This was in contrast to the experience of their less belligerent neighbors, the Mayo, who compensated by developing new religious movements and new legends that gave the people a sense of tribal identity. The Yaqui, meanwhile, were preserving mythic lore that would be useful in maintaining Indianness when military strategies no longer sufficed.

The Loss of the Ancients, still being told in Yaqui villages, is one means of signaling the continuance of Yaqui values. When Yaqui speak of the ancients, or *surem*, alive today in the wilderness or the underground, they are implying that the power of their ancestors is still operative.

Stories themselves, by the mere fact of their having survived, may be prized as a form of resistance. As a Chatino traditionalist puts it, "We do not worship the church. What we worship is the mountain and the sun stone [a hilltop shrine where people leave offerings], and that way we keep our Chatino rituals, beliefs, traditions, and stories."

As elsewhere in the hemisphere, the disappearance of Indian lore in Middle America has been predicted or declared a fact many times. Yet it continues to demonstrate its vitality, reemerging in communities where it had been presumed lost.

Even in a national setting the old myths are valued—by a Spanish-speaking culture that preserves its Indian heritage in books and museums. Is this the Middle American mythology of the future? Or will the old stories continue to be handed down and re-created in local communities that maintain their independence? Today, nearly five hundred years after the Conquest, it is still too early to say.

Certainly independence, in the future as in the past, will remain a key to mythological strength both at the level of the native community and at the national level; and this is true not only in Middle America, but throughout the hemisphere. Wherever Indian people have managed to stay together, keeping outsiders at a distance, they have preserved the ability to create myth; and myth in turn, like language and other customs, has helped to preserve local pride, cohesiveness, and, in short, independence.

On a larger scale, these local resources add to the life of nations, helping them to assert themselves in the global community. As long as the Americas are independent of the rest of the world, or desire to be independent, they will cherish the myths that have grown from their soil. These, after all, are artifacts that no other region can claim. Like the land itself, they cannot be removed. Always at home, impervious to shifts in taste or intellectual fashion, the old myths—preserved, expanded, condensed, reworked—contribute their own essential ingredient to the spirit of the New World.

ceiba / the silk-cotton tree (*Ceiba pentandra*)

charro / a Mexican horseman or cowboy, typically dressed in a fancy outfit that includes a broad-brimmed hat, or sombrero

chayote / a garden vegetable of the gourd family, also called vegetable pear (*Sechium edule*)

Chicano / a Mexican living in the United States (the feminine form is Chicana)

codex / (1) any early manuscript of scholarly importance, or (2) a pre-Columbian manuscript, especially one that opens like an accordion or folding screen

copal / resin from any of various trees, burned as incense to please the gods

gourd-fruit tree / a tree bearing large gourdlike fruit, also called calabash or calabash tree (*Crescentia cujete*)

Ladino / a term used by Indians in Central America and southern Mexico to mean a Latin as opposed to an Indian; that is, a person identified with the Spanish-speaking culture even though he may have Indian blood (the feminine form is Ladina)

maguey / any of various species of the genus *Agave*, commonly called century plants, whose fiber is woven into mats and other articles

malanga / a garden vegetable (*Xanthosoma* sp.) grown for its potato-like tubers

manioc / an important garden vegetable (*Manihot* sp.), also called cassava, grown for its starchy tuberous roots (there are two kinds: the "sweet," which is nonpoisonous, and the "bitter," which must be rinsed and pressed before use)

159

milpa / a cornfield or vegetable garden

peccary / either of two species of wild pig (*Tayassu tajacu* and *T. pecari*) hunted for food and hides

quetzal / a bird of the trogon family (*Pharomachrus mocinno*), valued for its long green tailfeathers

sapodilla / the large sweet fruit of the sapodilla tree (*Achras zapota*), one of the most highly prized fruits of tropical America

tamale / bits of meat and cornmeal dough boiled in a cornhusk or banana-leaf covering, a dish for festive occasions

tobacco gourd / a small gourd filled with tobacco, carried by shamans, especially among the Huichol

tortilla / a thin round sheet of cornmeal dough cooked on a griddle, the essential food, or "bread," of Mesoamerica

troupial / any of several large yellow-and-black orioles native to Mexico and Central America

Intended primarily as an accompaniment to the text, these notes may also be used to verify the myth distribution patterns shown on the maps in Part Two (see notes to Part Two, below).

Most sources are identified only by author, date, volume number (if needed), and page number or numbers. For example, "Dyk 1959, 3–5 & 17" refers to pages 3–5 and 17 of Anne Dyk's *Mixteca Texts*, published in 1959; "Lumholtz 1987 2, 8" means volume 2, page 8, of Lumholtz's *Unknown Mexico*, edition of 1987. Full bibliographic entries on these and all other cited works can be traced in the section entitled References.

The abbreviation HMAI stands for Wauchope's *Handbook of Middle American Indians*.

Introduction

Page 0 / Bribri *historias*: Stone 1962, 51.

Page 0 / The Sun and the Fire called *zazanilli*: Sahagún 1950–82 bk. 7, 8.

Page 0 / Aesop's Fables called *zazanilli*: Kutscher et al. 1987.

Page 0 / Wisdom-word fables (*tlamachiliztlatolzazanilli*): Codex Chimalpopoca, line 1 of manuscript page 75.

Page 0 / Wisdom fables (*tlahmach-zaniltin*): López Avila 1984, 2.

Page 0 / Two categories of stories: Gossen 1974, 50–51 & 78–79 & 140–41 (Tzotzil); Laughlin 1977, 1 (Tzotzil); Carrasco 1952, 36–37 (Tarascan);

M. Redfield 1935, 4 (Yucatec); Burns 1983, 19–24 (Yucatec); Houwald and Rener 1984, 3 (Sumu); Portal 1986, 29 (Mazatec).

Page oo / Field workers met with resistance: Miller 1956, 3 & 9–10 (Mixe); Hagen 1943, 59 (Jicaque); Cowan 1946, 33 (Mazatec); La Farge 1947, 47 (Kanjobal).

Page oo / Eval u vach: Edmonson 1971, 7.

Page oo / Franz Boas: Boas 1912; see also Foster 1948, 377.

Page oo / Summer Institute of Linguistics: Stoll 1983.

Page oo / Quetzalcoatl's discovery of corn: Codex Chimalpopoca, manuscript page 77.

Page oo / Preserved in three Maya documents: Edmonson 1971, 146–47 (Popol Vuh); Recinos et al. 1953, 46 (Annals of the Cakchiquels); Thompson 1970, 350–51 (Book of Chilam Balam of Chumayel).

Page oo / Quetzalcoatl's descent to the underworld: Codex Chimalpopoca, manuscript pages 76–77; "Histoyre du Mechique" 1905, ch. 7; Mendieta 1971, ch. 1 of bk. 2.

Page oo / The Loss of the Ancients: sources for these variants can be traced in the notes to Part Two, myth v (see below).

Page oo / Kirchhoff's list: Kirchhoff 1952, 24–25.

Page oo / "My remembered country": from the poem "Flowers from the Volcano," translated by Darwin J. Flakoll in Crow 1988, 174–79.

Part One: The Storytellers

Page oo / A passage from The Flight of Quetzalcoatl: Codex Chimalpopoca, manuscript page 6.

Page oo / Tula as a place of legend: Sahagún 1950–82 bk. 3 (ch. 3) & bk. 10 (ch. 29).

Page oo / Birth of the sun at Teotihuacán: ibid. bk. 7 (ch. 2).

Page oo / Olmec mythic figures: Joralemon 1971, 90.

Page oo / Storytelling in northern Puebla: Taggart 1983.

Page oo / Published storytellers of Milpa Alta: Horcasitas and Ford 1979, 170; López Avila 1984.

Page oo / Handmade books of the Otomi: Sandstrom and Sandstrom 1986.

Page oo / "These were the ones who lived far away": translated from the Nahuatl in Sahagún 1950–82 bk. 10 (ch. 29), 171.

Page oo / Huichol storytelling customs: Lumholtz 1987 2, 8; Myerhoff 1974, 97 & 108 & 142; HMAI 8, 808 & 810.

Page oo / "Who knows? Maybe someone will work sorcery": Zingg 1977, liii.

Page oo / Montezuma and the Mixtec woman: Codex Chimalpopoca, manuscript page 51; see also Durán 1967 2, 191–95 (ch. 22); HMAI 3, 968.

Page oo / Codex Vienna: J. Furst 1978.

Page oo / Chatino storytelling: Bartolomé 1979, 11–17; HMAI 7, 365.

Page oo / George Foster among the Popoluca: Foster 1945a.

Page oo / María Sabina: Estrada 1981.

Page oo / Mazatec wakes and storytelling: Portal 1986, 38; Laughlin 1971; Estrada 1981, 79 & 99; HMAI 7, 521–22.

Page oo / Chilam Balam books still in use: Burns 1977, 261–62; Burns 1983, 22–23; Bricker 1981–85 3, 53.

Page oo / Yucatec storytelling customs: M. Redfield 1935, 3–8; Burns 1983, 19–24.

Page oo / "Let's Hunt." "My rifle's broken": Burns 1983, 18, by permission of the University of Texas Press.

Page oo / "When I came along," "When I passed by": Andrade 1977, nos. 5 & 37 & 38 & 41; Bierhorst 1986, 143; see also Fought 1972, 144 (Chorti Maya).

Page oo / Tales portraying the Lacandon as cannibals: Tax 1949, 133; La Farge 1947, 67.

Page oo / Elaborate mythology of the Lacandon: Cline 1944; Bruce 1974; Boremanse 1986.

Page oo / Abbreviated and teaching versions of Lacandon stories: Bruce 1976, 16.

Page oo / Tzeltalan storytelling customs: Laughlin 1977, 5.

Page oo / Two major Tzotzil collections: Laughlin 1977; Gossen's collection, not yet fully published, is described in Gossen 1974.

Page oo / On the unity of Zinacantan narrative lore: Laughlin 1977, 4; but cf. ibid., 1 ("ancient" and "recent").

Page oo / "There is a story of long, long ago": Gossen 1974, 148–49. Reprinted by permission, © 1974 by the President and Fellows of Harvard College.

Page oo / Couplets in Lacandon, Cakchiquel, and other Maya narratives: Bierhorst 1986, 16; Edmonson 1971, xi-xii; Tedlock 1983, 143 & 220–29; Bricker 1981–85 3.

Page oo / Maya vase paintings related to mythology: Coe 1973; Coe 1978; Tedlock 1985; Schele and Miller 1986.

Page oo / Storytelling customs among the Guatemalan Maya: La Farge and Byers 1931, 112; Tedlock 1983, 247–48; Bricker 1981–85 3, 141.

Page oo / Victor Montejo and Adrián Chávez: Montejo 1985; Montejo n.d.; Chávez 1979.

Page oo / Crisis in Guatemala: Carmack 1988.

Page oo / Sixteenth-century reports from the Nicarao: Oviedo 1959 4, 363–75 (pt. 3, bk. 4, chs. 1–2).

Page oo / Myth of the girl from Guatemala: Chapman 1985, 86.

Page oo / The Dying God and Flute Lure: Bierhorst 1985b, 79 & 94–96 & 100–104 & 241.

Page oo / Kiliwa mythology: Ochurte and Mixco 1977; Mixco 1983.

Page oo / Mythology of the Paipai (also called Akwa'ala): Gifford and Lowie 1928, 350–51; Mixco 1977.

Page oo / Clavigero on the Cochimí, Guaicura, and Pericu: Clavigero 1971, 108–112 (bk. 1, ch. 24).

Page oo / Seri just-so stories: Kroeber 1931, 12–13.

Page oo / Reminiscent of the creation tales of central California: Kroeber 1931, 13; cf. Bierhorst 1985b, 116.

Page oo / Seri stories of ancient giants and of an arduous trail to the land of the dead: Griffen 1959, 19 & 21.

Page oo / Myths collected by Carl Lumholtz: Lumholtz 1987 1, 295–310.

Page oo / On the reported decline of Tarahumara mythology: Bennett and Zingg 1935, 365; Zingg 1942, 89.

Page oo / Storytelling at Cerocahui: Irigoyen Rascón 1974, 81.

Page oo / "Oh yes! That's a prayer": Irigoyen Rascón 1974, 120–21.

Page oo / Yaqui storytelling customs: Giddings 1959, 15–20.

Page oo / *Inkarrí*: Bierhorst 1988, 235–37 & 239.

Page oo / Story of White Buffalo Calf Woman: Bierhorst 1985b, 178–80.

Page oo / Works by Refugio Savala and Felipe Molina: Savala 1980; Evers and Molina 1987.

Page oo / The Tree and the Flood: Bierhorst 1988, passim.

Page oo / The Parrot Brides: Villanueva and Cubero 1983 (Cabécar); "Historias recogidas" 1984, 33 (Bribri); Stone 1962, 59 (Cabécar); cf. Bierhorst 1988, 20 & 114 & 216–17 & 239.

Page oo / The loathly god: R. Morales Stewart 1987, 18 (Bribri); Bozzoli 1979, 172 (Bribri); Septimo and Joly 1986, 11 (Guaymí); cf. Bierhorst 1988, 204 & 237.

Page oo / Origin of soil: Stone 1962, 53 (Cabécar); Pereira 1983, 46 (Bribri); Bozzoli 1979, 186–87 (Bribri); cf. Bierhorst 1988, 180.

Page oo / Iroquois observers at peace parley: *National Geographic*, Sept. 1987, p. 385.

Page oo / Russell Means in Central America: *New York Times*, Nov. 11, 1985, p. A3.

Page oo / ". . . the people suffer in your jungle": Henson 1987, 29.

Page oo / "The narrator starts slowly": translated from the Spanish-German text in Houwald and Rener 1984, 3 & 15.

Page oo / "They made a big circle": translated from the Spanish of Carlos Cuadra Pasos as quoted in Houwald and Rener 1984, 9.

Pages oo–oo / On the Jicaque and their mythology: Chapman 1982.

Page oo / Myths sung among Bribri and Guaymí: Bozzoli 1979, 29; Alphonse 1956, 125.

Page oo / Boruca storytelling customs: Constenla Umaña 1979, 44–45.

Pages oo–oo / "We who are Bribri": translated from the Spanish in Pereira 1983, 13–14, by permission of the University of Costa Rica.

Part Two: The Basic Myths

Page oo / myth i, The Emergence of Ancestors (Aztec): Mengin 1939, 100–2. Variants: Durán 1967 2, ch. 1 (Aztec); Kirchhoff et al. 1976, folio 16r

(Aztec); J. Furst 1978, 21 (Mixtec); Grigsby n.d., 2 & 6–7 & 14 (Nahua of Morelos and D.F.); Thompson 1970, 202 (Tzotzil).

Page oo / Headgear (*cozoyahualolli*): see Sahagún 1950–82 bk. 10, 172 & 173.

Page oo / Prayer mats (*tlemacuextli*, literally "incense-burner mat," from *tlemaitl* and *cuextli*): for rituals involving mats and incense burners, see Sahagún 1950–82 bk. 2, ch. 25.

Page oo / myth ii, The Man of Crops (Jicaque): Chapman 1982, 73–74, by permission of Instituto Nacional de Antropología e Historia. Variants: "Histoyre du Mechique" 1905, ch. 9 (Aztec); Alcorn 1984, 205 & 354 & 365 & 392 (Huastec); Myerhoff 1974, 213–14 (Huichol); González Casanova 1965, 99–105 (Nahua of Morelos and D.F.); Sandstrom n.d., 1–11 (Nahua of northern Veracruz and adjacent territory); Foster 1945a, 192 (Popoluca); Tax 1949, 127 (Quiché); Acevedo Barba et al. 1982, 97–100 (Tarascan); Mason 1914, 160 (Tepecano); Williams García 1972, 87–92 (Tepehua); Gossen 1974, 308 & 327 & 328–29 & 334–35 & 342–43 (Tzotzil).

Page oo / myth iii, Why the Earth Eats the Dead (Bribri): Pereira 1983, 46–48, by permission of the University of Costa Rica. Variants: Shaw 1971, 51–52 (Achi); "Histoyre du Mechique" 1905, ch. 7 (Aztec); Shaw 1971, 104 (Chuj); Preuss 1912, 145 & 146 (Cora); Septimo and Joly 1986, 11–25 (Guaymí); Chapman 1982, 127 & 129 & 130 (Jicaque); Crumrine 1973, 1143 (Mayo); Portal 1986, 45 (Mazatec); cf. Parsons 1936, 215–16 (Zapotec).

Page oo / myth iv, Opossum Steals Fire (Mazatec): Incháustegui 1977, 67–68, by permission of Instituto Nacional de Antropología e Historia. Variants: Bartolomé 1979, 28 (Chatino); Preuss 1912, 178–81 & 271–72 (Cora); Zingg 1977, 515 (Huichol); Cruz 1946, 217–18 (Mixtec); Taggart 1983, 103–4 (Nahua of northern Puebla); Williams García 1972, 67 (Tepehua); E. Hollenbach 1977, 142 (Trique).

Page oo / myth v, The Loss of the Ancients (Tarahumara): Irigoyen Rascón 1974, 112–13. Variants: Shaw 1971, 54 (Achi); Codex Chimalpopoca, manuscript pages 1–2 & 75 (Aztec); Moreno de los Arcos 1967 (Aztec); Stone 1962, 56 (Bribri); Vázquez 1979, 93 (Bribri); "Historias aportadas" 1984, 10 (Bribri); "Historias recogidas" 1984, 29 (Bribri); Merrifield 1967 (Chinantec); Weitlaner 1977, 224 & 226 (Chinantec); Anderson 1957, 313–14 (Chol); Fought 1972, 377–78 (Chorti); Alcorn 1984, 60 (Huastec); Colby and Colby 1981, 165–68 (Ixil); La Farge and Byers 1931, 113 (Jacaltec); Chapman 1982, 55 & 63–64 (Jicaque); Siegel 1943, 124 (Kanjobal); HMAI 7, 295 (Lacandon); Chapman 1985, 93–94 (Lenca); Oakes 1951, 234 (Mam); Incháustegui 1977, 212–13 (Mazatec); Dyk 1959, 3–5 & 17 (Mixtec); Ziehm 1968–76 1, 150–51 (Nahua of Durango); Taggart 1983, 89 & 192–93 (Nahua of northern Puebla); Schultze Jena 1935, 94–97 (Pipil); Reina 1966, 1–2 (Pokomam); Tedlock 1985, 78–86 & 178–82 (Quiché); Griffen 1959, 19 (Seri); Carrasco 1952, 38–39 (Tarascan); Mason 1914, 148–49 (Tepecano); HMAI 8, 671 (Totonac); Toor 1947, 483 (Tzeltal); Gossen 1974, 148–53 & 313–14 & 323–24 & 335 & 337 & 342 & 346

(Tzotzil); Laughlin 1977, 76–77 (Tzotzil); Thompson 1970, 344–46 (Tzotzil); Evers 1980, 190 (Yaqui); Evers and Molina 1987, 37–38 (Yaqui); Giddings 1959, 25–27 (Yaqui); Savala 1980, 39–43 (Yaqui); Spicer 1940, 240 (Yaqui); Spicer 1954, 121 (Yaqui); Spicer 1980, 172 (Yaqui); Toor 1947, 495 (Yaqui); Burns 1983, 52–60 (Yucatec); M. Redfield 1935, 24 (Yucatec); R. Redfield and Villa Rojas 1934, 12 & 330–31 (Yucatec); Roys 1967, 98–101 (Yucatec); Villa Rojas 1945, 153 (Yucatec); Leslie 1960, 21–22 (Zapotec); Parsons 1936, 216–17 & 220 & 327 & 340 & 341 (Zapotec).

Page oo / myth vi, The Flood Myth (Mixe): Lehmann 1928, 753–54 & 762–63. Variants: Codex Chimalpopoca, manuscript pages 75–76 (Aztec); Codex Vaticanus 3738, plate V (Aztec); Horcasitas 1988, 198 & 207 (Chol); Lumholtz 1987 2, 193–94 (Cora); Preuss 1912, 200–1 & 277–78 (Cora); Alcorn 1984, 60–61 & 92 (Huastec); Furst and Nahmad 1972, plate [18] (Huichol); Lumholtz 1987 2, 191–93 (Huichol); Preuss 1932, 452–53 & 454 (Huichol); McIntosh 1949–57, 15–19 (Huichol); Straatman 1988, 87–91 (Huichol); Zingg 1977, 539 (Huichol); Lehmann 1928, 754–57 (Mixe); Dyk 1959, 6–9 (Mixtec); Shaw 1971, 180–81 (Mopan); Ziehm 1968–76 1, 135–38 (Nahua of Durango); Taggart 1983, 194–97 (Nahua of northern Puebla); Horcasitas 1978, 184 (Nahua of northern Veracruz and adjacent territory); Stiles 1985a, 98–118 (Nahua of northern Veracruz and adjacent territory); Stiles 1985b, 18–25 (Nahua of northern Veracruz and adjacent territory); Paredes 1970, 3–4 (Otomi of Puebla); Foster 1945a, 235–39 (Popoluca); Carrasco 1952, 39 (Tarascan); Mason 1914, 163–64 (Tepecano); Horcasitas 1988, 198 (Tepehua); Williams García 1972, 79–80 (Tepehua); Lemley 1949–57, 76–78 (Tlapanec); Horcasitas 1988, 197 & 205–6 (Totonac); B. Hollenbach 1982 (Trique); Horcasitas 1988, 198 (Tzeltal); Gossen 1974, 320–21 & 342 (Tzotzil); M. Redfield 1935, 24–25 (Yucatec).

Page oo / myth vii, The Seeds of Humanity (Guaymí): Serrano y Sanz 1908, 88–89. Variants: Bozzoli 1979, 42 & 152 & 163 & 165 & 167–69 (Bribri); "Historias aportadas" 1984, 11 (Bribri); "Historias recopiladas" 1987, 31 (Bribri); Lehmann 1920 1, 334–35 (Bribri); R. Morales Stewart 1987, 18–19 (Bribri); Pereira 1983, 25 (Bribri); Pittier de Fábrega 1903, 2–3 & 3–4 (Bribri); Stone 1962, 53–54 & 57–58 (Cabécar); Lehmann 1920 1 (Guatuso); Septimo and Joly 1986, 11–25 (Guaymí); Steward 1948, 227–28 (Paya); cf. Gossen 1974, 335 (Tzotzil).

Page oo / myth viii, The Tree and the Flood (Cabécar): Stone 1962, 56–57, by permission of the Peabody Museum of Archaeology and Ethnology. Variants: "Historias aportadas" 1984, 7–8 (Bribri); Stone 1962, 56 (Bribri); Vázquez 1979, 93–94 (Bribri); Stone 1962, 53–54 (Cabécar); cf. Oakes 1951, 234 (Mam); cf. Thompson 1930, 134–35 (Mopan)

Page oo / myth ix, The Hidden Corn (Mopan): Thompson 133. Variants: Shaw 1971, 41–42 (Achi); Codex Chimalpopoca, manuscript page 77 (Aztec); Recinos et al. 1953, 46–47 (Cakchiquel); R. Redfield 1945, 36 (Cakchiquel); Fought 1972, 185 (Chorti); Alcorn 1984, 62–63 & 82 & 90 & 207 (Huastec);

Montejo n.d. (Jacaltec); Burkitt 1920 (Kekchi); Furbee-Losee 1976–80 1, 95 (Mam); Miles 1960 (Mam); Petrich 1985, 292–93 (Motozintlec); Taggart 1983, 89–92 (Nahua of northern Puebla); Stiles 1985a, 106–7 (Nahua of northern Veracruz and adjacent territory); Schultze Jena 1935, 30–35 (Pipil); Mayers 1958, 6–12 & 12–15 (Pokomchi); Thompson 1970, 350 (Pokomchi); Tedlock 1985, 163 & 251 (Quiché); Nash 1970, 43 & 44 & 326–27 (Tzeltal); Slocum 1965, 2–7 (Tzeltal); Thompson 1970, 350–51 (Yucatec).

Page oo / myth x, Corn Woman's Marriage (Cora): Preuss 1912, 182–89. Variants: Myerhoff 1974, 210–13 (Huichol); Preuss 1907, 185–90 (Huichol); Toor 1947, 499 (Huichol); Zingg 1977, 535–37 (Huichol); Ziehm 1968–76 1, 164–71 (Nahua of Durango); Mason 1914, 155–62 & 204–5 (Tepecano).

Page oo / Huichol myth told with much weeping: Myerhoff 1974, 213.

Page oo / [And would trade them for corn]: as in the Huichol variant in Zingg 1977, 535.

Page oo / myth xi, The Grasshoppers and the Corn (Pipil): Schultze Jena 105–6. Variants: Bartolomé 1979, 29 (Chatino); La Farge and Byers 1931, 126 (Jacaltec); Horcasitas 1978, 183 (Nahua of southern Veracruz).

Page oo / myth xii, The Sun and the Fire (Huichol): Lumholtz 1987 2, 107–8. Variants: Bierhorst 1984, 135 (Aztec); Codex Chimalpopoca, manuscript pages 77–78 (Aztec); Coe and Whittaker 1982, 100–2 (Aztec); cf. Septimo and Joly 1986, 11–25 (Guaymí); Alcorn 1984, 58 (Huastec); Horcasitas 1978, 183 (Nahua of Morelos and D.F.); Taggart 1983, 101–2 (Nahua of northern Puebla); Conzemius 1932, 130 (Sumu); HMAI 8, 671 (Totonac).

Page oo / myth xiii, How the Sun Was Named (Yaqui): Giddings 1959, 34, by permission of the University of Arizona Press, copyright 1959. Variants: Preuss 1912, 143 (Cora); Zingg 1977, 517–18 (Huichol); Ziehm 1968–76 1, 145–49 (Nahua of Durango).

Page oo / myth xiv, The Childhood of Sun and Moon (Chatino): Bartolomé 1979, 23–25, by permission of Instituto Nacional de Antropología e Historia. Variants: De Cicco and Horcasitas 1962 (Chatino); Carrasco and Weitlaner 1949–57, 169–73 (Chinantec); Weitlaner 1977, 52–55 (Chinantec); Weitlaner 1977, 56–62 (Cuicatec); Incháustegui 1977, 27–34 (Mazatec); Portal 1986, 49–57 (Mazatec); Carrasco and Weitlaner 1949–57, 168–69 (Mixe); Hoogshagen 1971 (Mixe); Miller 1956, 75–98 (Mixe); Dyk 1959, 10–16 (Mixtec); Barlow and Ramírez 1962 (Nahua of southern Veracruz); Foster 1945a, 217 (Popoluca); E. Hollenbach 1977 (Trique); Parsons 1936, 324–27 (Zapotec); Stubblefield and Stubblefield 1969 (Zapotec).

Page oo / myth xv, Sun and His Brothers (Tzotzil): Laughlin 1977, 40–41. Variants: R. Redfield 1945, 252–54 (Cakchiquel); Thompson 1970, 362–63 (Chol); Shaw 1971, 101–4 (Chuj); Shaw 1971, 138–42 (Jacaltec); Siegel 1943, 121–24 (Kanjobal); Dieseldorff 1926, 5 (Kekchi); Thompson 1930, 119–25 (Mopan); Tedlock 1985, 119–24 (Quiché); Slocum 1965, 8–18

167

(Tzeltal); Gossen 1974, 312 & 325–26 & 338 (Tzotzil); Guiteras-Holmes 1961, 183–86 (Tzotzil); Laughlin 1977, 387–88 (Tzotzil); cf. Shaw 1971, 239 (Tzutujil).

Page oo / myth xvi, The Courtship of Sun and Moon (Kekchi): Shaw 1971, 153–55, by permission of the Summer Institute of Linguistics. Variants: R. Redfield 1945, 291–370 (Cakchiquel); Furbee-Losee 1976–80, 60–66 (Ixil); Colby and Colby 1981, 180–83 (Ixil); Dieseldorff 1926, 4–5 (Kekchi); Gordon 1915, 120–21 (Kekchi); Shaw 1971, 175–79 (Mopan); Thompson 1930, 126–29 (Mopan); Mayers 1958, 3–6 (Pokomchi).

Page oo / myth xvii, Thunder's Apprentice (Mam): P. Morales 1977, 10. Variants: R. Redfield 1945, 134–36 (Cakchiquel); Thompson 1930, 146–50 (Mopan); Madsen 1960, 131–32 (Nahua of Morelos and D.F.); Williams García 1972, 81 (Tepehua); cf. Gossen 1974, 341 (Tzotzil); Andrade 1977, story no. 1 (Yucatec); Villa Rojas et al. 1975 as reprinted in Scheffler 1985, 87–92 (Zoque).

Page oo / myth xviii, The Dead Wife (Mískito): Conzemius 1932, 159–60. Variants: Zingg 1977, 544–46 (Huichol); Chapman 1982, 241–42 (Jicaque); Bruce 1974, 258–74 (Lacandon); Ziehm 1968–76 1, 263–72 (Nahua of Durango); Vázquez 1982 (Nahua of northern Puebla); Mason 1914, 208 (Tepecano); E. Hollenbach 1980, 456–57 (Trique); Maurer Avalos and Guzmán 1985 (Tzeltal); Toor 1947, 479–81 (Tzeltal); Laughlin 1977, 28–30 & 70–71 (Tzotzil); Burns 1983, 121–34 (Yucatec); Parsons 1936, 362–63 (Zapotec).

Page oo / myth xix, The Buzzard Husband (Tzutujil): Orellana 1975, 856–58, by permission of Anthropos Institute. Variants: Shaw 1971, 64 (Aguacatec); Schoembs 1905, 221–22 (Cakchiquel); Tax 1950, no. 7 (Cakchiquel); Furbee-Losee 1976–80 1, 30 (Kekchi); Applebaum 1967, 79–80 (Mam); Dyk 1959, 115–23 (Mixtec); Ziehm 1968–76 1, 272–74 (Nahua of Durango); Taggart 1983, 208–11 (Nahua of northern Puebla); Lemley 1949–57, 81–82 (Tlapanec); E. Hollenbach 1980, 457–58 (Trique); Gossen 1974, 314–15 (Tzotzil); Guiteras-Holmes 1961, 204 (Tzotzil); Laughlin 1977, 50–51 & 246–51 & 342–43 (Tzotzil); Giddings 1959, 59 (Yaqui).

Page oo / myth xx, The Visit to the Animal Master (Chinantec): Weitlaner 1977, 116–17, by permission of Instituto Nacional Indigenista. Variants: Pittier de Fábrega 1903, 7–8 (Boruca); Constenla Umaña 1979, 178–79 (Boruca); Stone 1962, 64 (Bribri); "Historias aportadas" 1984, 10 (Bribri); Kunst, 1915, 355 (Chuj); Furbee-Losee 1976–80 3, 69–78 (Ixil); Colby and Colby 1974, 217–21 (Ixil); Colby and Colby 1981, 175–76 (Ixil); Chapman 1982, 143–44 & 156–57 (Jicaque); Chapman 1985, 144–48 (Lenca); Stiles 1984 (Nahua of northern Veracruz and adjacent territory); Reyes García and Christensen 1976, 77–79 (Nahua of central Veracruz); Foster 1945a, 200–1 & 210–11 (Popoluca); Conzemius 1932, 166–67 (Sumu); Mason 1914, 153–55 (Tepecano); Williams García 1972, 117–18 (Tepehua); Gossen 1974, 299 (Tzotzil); Giddings 1959, 62 (Yaqui); Paredes 1970, 5–7 (Zoque).

Part Three: Building Mythologies

Page 000 / Myth of the animal farmers and the hidden corn: Taggart 1983, 89–91 (Nahua of northern Puebla); cf. Alcorn 1984, 62–63 (Huastec).

Page 000 / Modern Yucatec version of the myth of world ages: Tozzer 1907, 153–54.

Page 000 / Version preserved in the Annals of Cuauhtitlan: Codex Chimalpopoca, manuscript page 2.

Page 000 / Old Quiché version of the four creations: Tedlock 1985, 76–86 & 163–64.

Page 000 / Aztec version with pine nuts and wild corn: Moreno de los Arcos 1967, 205.

Page 000 / They had "small bodies and large brains": Redfield and Villa Rojas 1934, 330.

Page 000 / Gossen's collection of 92 "ancient" stories: Gossen 1974, 299–346.

Page 000 / "In the days when there was not yet a moon": Schultze Jena 1935, 93.

Page 000 / Creation cycle of the Pipil: Schultze Jena 1935, 22–35; a variant is in Hartman 1907.

Page 000 / the Bodiless Wife: Laughlin 1977, 65–66 & 179–82 & 301–5 & 320–21 & 333–34 & 372–73 (Tzotzil); Thompson 1930, 158 (Kekchi).

Page 000 / Skull-fruit story in the Popol Vuh: Tedlock 1985, 112–17.

Page 000 / Old Woman's Lover among the Mopan and the Kekchi: Thompson 1970, 355.

Page 000 / "Pipil thought focuses on four things": Schultze Jena 1935, 4.

Page 000 / Myths of Quetzalcoatl and Tezcatlipoca: "Histoyre du Mechique" 1905, ch. 7 (Why the Earth Eats the Dead); "History of the Mexicans as Told by Their Paintings" 1884, chs. 3–4 (The Loss of the Ancients); Codex Chimalpopoca, manuscript pages 75–76 (The Flood Myth); Codex Chimalpopoca, manuscript page 77 (The Hidden Corn); Boone 1983, 206 (origin of flowers); Bierhorst 1984, 37–38 (origin of music); "History of the Mexicans as Told by Their Paintings" 1884, ch. 5 (How the sky was raised).

Page 000 / Trique myth of the nine gods: Valentini 1899.

Page 000 / Nine gods and thirteen gods among the Aztecs and the ancient Maya: Nicholson 1971, tables 2 & 3 (Aztec); Thompson 1970, 280–82 (Maya).

Page 000 / Nine gods among the Zapotec: Weitlaner and de Cicco 1962.

Page 000 / Huichol myths of the wet and dry seasons: Zingg 1977, 515–55.

Page 000 / Myths of quartering the earth: "Histoyre du Mechique" 1905, ch. 7 (Aztec); Recinos et al. 1950, 80 (Quiché); Septimo and Joly 1986, 11–25 (Guaymí); "Historias aportadas" 1984, 7–8 (Bribri); Bozzoli 1979, 196 (Bribri).

Page 000 / World levels: Merrill 1983, 296 (Tarahumara); Merrill 1988, 71 (Tarahumara); Chapman 1982, 97 (Jicaque); Tozzer 1907, 154–56 (modern Yucatec); Nicholson 1971, table 2 (Aztec); Holland and Tharp 1964, 42 (Tzotzil); Thompson 1970, 195 (ancient Yucatec).

Page 000 / World as cube, earth's surface as square: HMAI 7, 175; Gossen 1980, 132.

Page 000 / Thompson's suggestion that Yucatec viewed the world as a rectangular box, or house: Thompson 1970, 214–15; cf. Barrera Vásquez et al. 1980, 272; see also Schele and Miller 1986, 45 & 54 & passim.

Page 000 / Guaymí conception of the world house: Septimo and Joly 1986, 19.

Page 000 / Sibu's house according to the Bribri: "Historias recogidas" 1984, 29 (Pleiades as pole tips); "Historias aportadas" 1984, 7 (tree threatens to break roof).

Page 000 / Lord Sun "placed a mirror in the center of the sky": Thompson 1930, 132.

Page 000 / Sun "rises in the morning, traverses till midday": "History of the Mexicans as Told by Their Paintings" 1884, ch. 3.

Page 000 / Stars shoot arrows at jaguars: Sandstrom and Sandstrom 1986, 204.

Page 000 / Myths of the origin of stars: Bruce 1974, ch. 9 (Lacandon); Chapman 1982, 55 & 110 (Jicaque); Stone 1962, 55 (Cabécar).

Page 000 / Location of the dead land: Bozzoli 1979, 133 & 157–58 (Bribri); Griffen 1959, 20 (Seri); Lehmann 1910, 717 (Mískito).

Page 000 / Souls climb tree to reach seventh heaven: Tozzer 1907, 154.

Page 000 / Aztec journey through eight underworld obstacles: Codex Vaticanus 3738, plate II; cf. Sahagún 1950–82, appendix ch. 1 of bk. 3.

Page 000 / Dead envisioned as birds, moths, or butterflies: Sahagún 1950–82, appendix ch. 3 of bk. 3 (Aztec); Merrill 1988, 113 (Tarahumara); Skinner 1920, 101 (Bribri); Part Two of this book, myth xviii (Mískito); HMAI 7:542 (Chinantec).

Page 000 / Lacandon obstacles are illusions that deceive the souls: Bruce 1974, 256–57.

Page 000 / Dog punishes the wicked: Conzemius 1927, 323 (Rama); Griffen 1959, 21 (Seri).

Page 000 / Punishment for mistreating a dog: Bruce 1974, 255 (Lacandon); Carrasco 1952, 41 (Tarascan).

Page 000 / Maya tombs "have yielded skeletons": Thompson 1970, 301.

Page 000 / Modern Nahua belief in three realms of the dead: Madsen 1960, 219 (Nahua of Distrito Federal); cf. Sahagún 1950–82, appendix chs. 1–3 of bk. 3 (Aztec); cf. Séjourné 1952, 26 (Otomi); cf. Guiteras-Holmes 1961, 159 (Tzotzil).

Page 000 / Tree of breasts: Codex Vaticanus 3738, plate IV (Aztec); Laughlin 1977, 29 (Tzotzil of Zinacatán); Thompson 1970, 301 (Tzotzil of Chamula).

Page 000 / Newborn children come from Mother Scorpion: Lehmann 1910, 717.

Page 000 / "Well, of course that happened in those days": Myerhoff 1974, 85.

Page 000 / Legend of Huitzilopochtli: Bierhorst 1984, 65–83 & 137–39.

Page 000 / Quetzalcoatl as heroic child: Codex Chimalpopoca, manuscript pages 3–4 & 80–81; Mendieta 1971, ch. 5 of bk. 2; "Histoyre du Mechique" 1905, ch. 10.

Page ooo / Stories of heroes hatched from eggs: Foster 1945a, 191–94 (Homshuk of the Popoluca); Miller 1956, 105–9 (Kondoy of the Mixe); HMAI 7, 559–60 (Fane Kansini of the Tequistlatec); González Cruz 1984 (Tamacasti of the Nahua of Southern Veracruz); cf. Paredes 1970, 7–22 (Kondoy and Tamacasti).

Page ooo / The Dwarf of Uxmal: Redfield and Villa Rojas 1934, 335–37. Variants: Stephens 1969 2, 423–25; Mediz Bolio 1983, 77–93;

Page ooo / The twins' victory provided a charm against the perils of the underworld: see Schele and Miller 1986, 32; cf. Coe 1978.

Page ooo / He Who Builds Fires: Coolidge and Coolidge 1971, ch. 12; Griffen 1959, 18; Kroeber 1931, 12.

Page ooo / Quetzalcoatl as wise instructor: Durán 1967 1, ch. 1; Mendieta 1971, ch. 10 of bk. 2; Sahagún 1950–82, ch. 3 of bk. 3.

Page ooo / Votan: Brinton 1970, 212–15.

Page ooo / Itzamná: Bancroft 1882, 463; Tozzer 1966, 145–46; Brinton 1970, 146–47.

Page ooo / Tioipitzintli: Antonio Tello as paraphrased in Gamiz 1948, 67–68; on Tello, see HMAI 13, 153–54.

Page ooo / Ulikron: Alphonse 1956, 125.

Page ooo / Flight of Quetzalcoatl: Codex Chimalpopoca, manuscript pages 5–8; Sahagún 1950–82, chs. 4–14 of bk. 3.

Page ooo / Life of Christ, Flight of Christ, Christ and the Farmer: for European, South American, and Maya sources, see Bierhorst 1988, 208–11 & 253; Bierhorst 1986, 148. Other Middle American variants: Crumrine 1973, 1128–30 & 1142–43 (Mayo); Laughlin 1971 (Mazatec); Ziehm 1968–76 1, 155–59 (Nahua of Durango); Gibson and Olson 1963, 126–30 (Pame—with ogress as Christ's pursuer); Elson 1945–48 (Popoluca—with Homshuk as Christ); Tax 1949, 127 (Quiché—with Christ as man of crops); Guiteras-Holmes 1961, 262–63 (Tzotzil—with Ohoroxtotil as Christ); Laughlin 1977, 334–35 (Tzotzil—with comparative notes).

Page ooo / Stories of Kauyumari: Zingg 1977, 529–30 (as dupe) & 535–46 (as hero in creation cycle).

Page ooo / European-style trickster stories told of Coyote, Rabbit, and other animal characters: see Foster 1945b, 229–35; Bierhorst 1986, 72–83 & 146.

Page ooo / Popoluca giants: Foster 1945a, 209.

Pages ooo / Gnomes with enormous ears: Weitlaner 1977, 134.

Page ooo / Kurupira: see Bierhorst 1988, 193–94 & 252.

Page ooo / Guerrero tale of Plumed Serpent: Carrasco 1945–48.

Page ooo / Ogress with huge ear: Hobgood 1970, 406.

Page ooo / *Xtabay*: Barrera Vásquez et al. 1980, 953 (Yucatec); Bruce 1974, 109–111 (Lacandon).

Pages ooo–oo / Description of the Popol Vuh is based on three English translations: Tedlock 1985, Edmonson 1971, and Recinos et al. 1950.

Pages 000–00 / Description of Legend of the Suns is based on Codex Chimalpopoca, manuscript pages 75–84.

Page 000 / On Tonantzin and Our Lady of Guadalupe: Sahagún 1950–82 Introductory Volume, 90 (Tonantzin-Guadalupe as Mother of the Gods); Sahagún 1950–82 bk. 1, ch. 8 (Mother of the Gods as patroness of healers); Sahagún 1969 bk. 1, ch. 6 (Tonantzin as Cihuacoatl, who wailed at night).

Page 000 / Story of Juan Diego and the Lady: Bierhorst 1984, 10–11 & 115–27 & 142–43.

Page 000 / "I have written your miracle . . .": Lasso 1926, 20 (onoconìcuilo nahuatlàtolcopa in motlamahuiçoltzin . . . çayè xicmopaccaçelili inic nomaçehuallàtolli).

Page 000 / Religious movement in Michoacán: *New York Times*, Nov. 12, 1982, p. A2.

Page 000 / Legend of the eagle and the serpent: Bierhorst 1984, 80–83.

Page 000 / "If there isn't but dust in the pot": Cardenal 1973, 17.

Page 000 / "A hero struggled against the lords": Cuadra 1988, 131.

Page 000 / "Today they are monkeys, apes, gorillas": Argueta 1987, 73.

Page 000 / "For Mexicans, death sees and touches itself": Paz 1979, 145.

Page 000 / Poem by Aurelio Ballados: Bustamente Rabago 1981, 37–45.

Page 000 / "Sorcerers tried to ridicule Quetzalcoatl": Codex Chimalpopoca, manuscript page 5.

Page 000 / "Nothing but bread and flowers": Mendieta 1971 bk. 2, ch. 10.

Page 000 / Nezahualcoyotl as heroic child: Codex Chimalpopoca, manuscript pages 36–39 (his miraculous rebirth and childhood exploits) & 45–47 (his ultimate victory).

Page 000 / Nezahualcoyotl descended from Quetzalcoatl: Ixtlilxóchitl 1, 282.

Page 000 / Nezahualcoyotl as poet and philosopher: Ixtlilxóchitl 1, 404–6 & 447; for critical discussion see Bierhorst 1985a, 103–5.

Page 000 / "He overthrew tyrants and military juntas": Cardenal 1973, 70.

Page 000 / Poem by Ricardo Sánchez: Rodríguez Prampolini 1983, 223–25.

Page 000 / Poem by Juan Felipe Herrera: Rodríguez Prampolini 1983, 220–21, by permission of Instituto de Investigaciones Estéticas, National University of Mexico.

Page 000 / Lord of Calvary: HMAI 8, 629.

Page 000 / Christ of Chamula: Pineda 1888, 70–118; Bricker 1979, 34–40; HMAI 7, 149–50.

Page 000 / Virgin of Cerro Amarillo: Riley and Hobgood 1959.

Page 000 / Virgin of the Guaymí: Young 1971, 212–24.

Page 000 / Montezuma in the Pueblos: Bierhorst 1985b, 106 & 242.

Page 000 / *Inkarrí*: Bierhorst 1988, 235–37 & 239 & 254.

Page 000 / Chatino king: Bartolomé 1979, 21–22 & cf. 40–45.

Page 000 / Montezuma of the Popoluca: Foster 1945, 215.

Page 000 / Cortés and the daughter of Montezuma: Bierhorst 1985a, 323 & 473; Bierhorst 1985c, 176.

Page ooo / Cuasrán: Constenla Umaña 1979, 36 & 170–73 & 178–79.

Page ooo / Maya king: Redfield and Villa Rojas 1934, 331–32.

Page ooo / Tecun Uman: Carmack 1973, 301–3 (in history); Shaw 1971, 223–24 (in legend); Carmack 1988, 69 (in the 1980s).

Page ooo / Return of dead kings in Aztec ritual: Bierhorst 1985a, 3–122 & 527 ("In these [songs] they speak of conspiracy against ourselves").

Page ooo / Demands made by Indian congresses in Mexico: Barre 1985, 122–36.

Page ooo / Mayo religious movements: Crumrine 1975; HMAI 8, 833–34 & 844.

Page ooo / "We do not worship the church": Bartolomé 1979, 21

REFERENCES

Hardly a complete bibliography of Middle American mythology, the following serves mainly to amplify the Notes on Sources, above. In an attempt to make it more useful, a dagger (†) has been added to any title that contains significant comparative notes or an important regional study, and an asterisk (*) denotes an unusually full collection of stories from a particular culture.

An up-to-date bibliography of Middle American Indians is much needed. Until it appears, scholars are using a number of older lists, including those in Wauchope's *Handbook of Middle American Indians*, vols. 8 and 15, as well as Bernal's *Bibliografía de arqueología y etnografía*. Useful lists of works on mythology are in Foster's "The Current Status of Mexican Indian Folklore Studies" and Laughlin's *Of Cabbages and Kings* (see below).

The following abbreviations have been used throughout: INAH (Instituto Nacional de Antropología e Historia), JAF (*Journal of American Folklore*), and UNAM (Universidad Nacional Autónoma de México).

Acevedo Barba, Cruz R., et al. *Mitos de la meseta tarasca: un análisis estructural.* Mexico: UNAM, 1982.

Alcorn, Janis B. *Huastec Mayan Ethnobotany.* Austin: University of Texas Press, 1984.

Alphonse, Ephraim S. *Guaymí Grammar and Dictionary with Some Ethnological Notes.* Bureau of American Ethnology, Bulletin 162. 1956.

Anderson, Arabelle. "Two Chol Texts," *Tlalocan* 3 (1957): 313–16.

Andrade, Manuel J. "Yucatec Maya Stories," Microfilm Collection of Manuscripts on Cultural Anthropology, no. 262. Joseph Regenstein Library, University of Chicago. 1977.

Applebaum, Richard P. *San Ildefonso Ixtahuacan, Guatemala.* Cuadernos, ser. 3, no. 17. Seminario de Integración Social Guatemalteca, 1967.

Argueta, Manlio. *Cuzcatlán* (trans. Clark Hansen). New York: Random House / Vintage, 1987.

Bancroft, Hubert Howe. *Works,* vol. 3 (= *The Native Races,* vol. 3: Myths and Languages). San Francisco: A. L. Bancroft, 1882.

Barlow, R. H., and Valentin Ramírez. "Tonatiw iwan meetstli," *Tlalocan* 4 (1962): 55–61.

Barre, Marie-Chantal. *Ideologías indigenistas y movimientos indios.* 2d ed. Mexico: Siglo Veintiuno, 1985.

Barrera Vásquez et al. *Diccionario maya Cordemex.* Mérida, Yucatán: Ediciones Cordemex, 1980.

Bartolomé, Miguel Alberto. *Narrativa y etnicidad entre los chatinos de Oaxaca.* Mexico: INAH, 1979.

Bennett, Wendell C., and Robert M. Zingg. *The Tarahumara.* Chicago: University of Chicago Press, 1935.

Bernal, Ignacio. *Bibliografía de arqueología y etnografía: Mesoamérica y norte de México,* 1514–1960. Mexico: INAH, 1962.

Bierdermann, Hans. *Altmexikos heilige Búcher.* Graz, Austria: Akademische Druck) und Verlagsanstalt, 1971.

Bierhorst, John, ed. *Cantares Mexicanos: Songs of the Aztecs.* Stanford, Calif.: Stanford University Press, 1985. Cited as Bierhorst 1985a.

———. *The Hungry Woman: Myths and Legends of the Aztecs.* New York: Morrow, 1984.

———. *The Monkey's Haircut and Other Stories Told by the Maya.* New York: Morrow, 1986.

———. *The Mythology of North America.* New York: Morrow, 1985. Cited as Bierhorst 1985b.

———. *The Mythology of South America.* New York: Morrow, 1988.

———. *A Nahuatl-English Dictionary and Concordance to the Cantares Mexicanos.* Stanford, Calif.: Stanford University Press, 1985. Cited as Bierhorst 1985c.

Boas, Franz. "Notes on Mexican Folkore," JAF 25 (1912): 204–60.

Boone, Elizabeth Hill. *The Codex Magliabechiano and the Lost Prototype of the Magliabechiano Group.* Berkeley: University of California Press, 1983.

*Boremanse, Didier. *Contes et mythologie des indiens lacandons.* Paris: L'Harmattan, 1986.

Bozzoli, María E. *El nacimiento y la muerte entre los bribris.* San José: Universidad de Costa Rica, 1979.

Bricker, Victoria R. "Movimientos religiosos indígenas en los altos de Chiapas," *América Indígena* 39 (1979): 17–46.

———, ed. *Supplement to the Handbook of Middle American Indians.* 3 vols. Austin: University of Texas Press, 1981–85.

Brinton, Daniel G. *American Hero-Myths.* New York: Johnson Reprint, 1970.

176

*Bruce, Robert D. *El libro de Chan K'in*. Mexico: INAH, 1974.

———. *Textos y dibujos lacandones de Naja / Lacandon texts and drawings from Nahá*. Mexico: INAH, 1976.

Burkitt, Robert. *The Hills and the Corn: A Legend of the Kekchi Indians of Guatemala*. . . . Anthropological Publications of the University Museum, vol. 8, no. 2. Philadelphia: University of Pennsylvania, 1920.

Burns, Allan F. "The Caste War in the 1970s," *Anthropology and History in Yucatán* (ed. Grant D. Jones), 259–74. Austin: University of Texas Press, 1977.

———. *An Epoch of Miracles: Oral Literature of the Yucatec Maya*. Austin: University of Texas Press, 1983.

Bustamente Rabago, Fernando, comp. *Cuadernos tuxtecos* 4: recopilación poética de Santiago Tuxtla, San Andrés Tuxtla y Catemaco. Mexico: INAH, 1981.

Cardenal, Ernesto. *Homage to the American Indians* (trans. Monique and Carlos Altschul). Baltimore: Johns Hopkins University Press, 1973.

Carmack, Robert, ed. *Harvest of Violence: The Maya Indians and the Guatemalan Crisis*. Norman: University of Oklahoma Press, 1988.

———. *Quichean Civilization*. Berkeley: University of California Press, 1973.

Carrasco, Pedro. "Quetzalcoatl, dios de Coatepec de los Costales, Gro.," *Tlalocan* 2 (1945–48): 89–91.

———. *Tarascan Folk Religion*. New Orleans: Middle American Research Institute, Tulane University, 1952.

———, and Roberto J. Weitlaner. "El sol y la luna," *Tlalocan* 3 (1949–57): 168–74.

Caso, Alfonso. *The Aztecs: People of the Sun*. Norman: University of Oklahoma Press, 1958.

*Chapman, Anne. *Los hijos de la muerte: el universo mítico de los Tolupan-Jicaques (Honduras)*. Mexico: INAH, 1982.

———. *Los hijos del copal y la candela: ritos agrarios y tradición oral de los lencas de Honduras*. Mexico: UNAM, 1985.

Chávez, Adrián I. *Pop Wuj*. Mexico: Ediciones de la Casa Chata, 1979.

Clavigero, Francisco Javier. *The History of (Lower) California* (trans. Sara E. Lake). Riverside, Calif.: Manessier, 1971.

Cline, Howard. "Lore and Deities of the Lacandon Indians, Chiapas, Mexico," *JAF* 57 (1944): 107–15.

Codex Chimalpopoca. Nahuatl transcription and English translation prepared by John Bierhorst, based on the manuscript facsimile in Velázquez 1945 (see below). Typescript. Publication forthcoming.

Codex Vaticanus 3738. In *Antigüedades de México, basadas en la recopilación de Lord Kingsborough* (ed. Antonio Ortiz Mena, Agustín Yáñez, and José Corona Núñez), vol. 3. Mexico: Secretaría de Hacienda y Crédito Pública, 1964.

Códice Borgia. Mexico: Fondo de Cultura Económica, 1963.

Coe, Michael D. *Lords of the Underworld: Masterpieces of Maya Ceramics*. Princeton, N.J.: Princeton University Press, 1978.

———. *The Maya Scribe and His World*. New York: Grolier Club, 1973.

———, and Gordon Whittaker. *Aztec Sorcerers in Seventeenth Century Mexico: The*

177

Treatise on Superstitions by Hernando Ruiz de Alarcón. State University of New York at Albany, Institute for Mesoamerican Studies, 1982.

Colby, Benjamin N., and Lore M. Colby. *The Daykeeper: The Life and Discourse of an Ixil Diviner*. Cambridge, Mass.: Harvard University Press, 1981.

———. "Two Ixil Myths," *Anthropos* 69 (1974): 216–23.

Constenla Umaña, Adolfo. *Leyendas y tradiciones borucas*. Narradas por Espíritu Santo Maroto. San José: Universidad de Costa Rica, 1979.

Conzemius, Eduard. *Ethnographical Survey of the Miskito and Sumu Indians of Honduras and Nicaragua*. Bureau of American Ethnology, Bulletin 106. 1932.

———. "Die Rama-Indianer von Nicaragua," *Zeitschrift fúr Ethnologie* 59 (1927): 291–362.

Coolidge, Dane, and Mary R. Coolidge. *The Last of the Seris*. Glorieta, N. Mex.: Rio Grande Press, 1971.

Cowan, Florencia Hausen. "Notas etnográficas sobre los mazatecos de Oaxaca, Méx.," *América Indígena* 6 (1946): 27–39.

Crow, Mary, ed. *Woman Who Has Sprouted Wings: Poems by Contemporary Latin American Women Poets*. Pittsburgh: Latin American Literary Review Press, 1988.

Crumrine, N. Ross. "A New Mayo Indian Religious Movement in Northwest Mexico," *Journal of Latin American Lore* 1 (1975): 127–45.

———. "La tierra te devorará: un análisis estructural de los mitos de los indígenas mayo," *América Indígena* 33 (1973): 1119–50.

Cruz, Wilfrido C. *Oaxaca recóndita*. Mexico, 1946.

Cuadra, Pablo Antonio. *The Birth of the Sun* (trans. Steven F. White). Greensboro, North Carolina: Unicorn, 1988.

de Cicco, Gabriel, and Fernando Horcasitas. "Los Cuates: un mito chatino," *Tlalocan*, 4 (1962): 74–79.

Dieseldorff, E. P. *Kunst und Religion der Mayavölker*. Berlin: Julius Springer, 1926.

Durán, Diego de. *Historia de las Indias de Nueva España e islas de la tierra firme* (ed. Angel M. Garibay K.) Vol. 1: *Libro de los ritos y ceremonias . . .* and *El calendario antiguo*. Vol. 2: *Historia*. Mexico: Porrúa, 1967.

Dyk, Anne. *Mixteca Texts*. Norman: Summer Institute of Linguistics of the University of Oklahoma, 1959.

Edmonson, Munro S., trans. *The Book of Counsel: The Popol Vuh of the Quiche Maya of Guatemala*. New Orleans: Middle American Research Institute, Tulane University, 1971.

Elson, Ben. "The Homshuk: A Sierra Popoluca Text," *Tlalocan*, 2 (1945–48): 193–214.

Estrada, Alvaro. *María Sabina: Her Life and Chants*. With translations by Henry Munn. Santa Barbara, Calif.: Ross-Erikson, 1981.

Evers, Larry, ed. *The South Corner of Time: Hopi, Navajo, Papago, Yaqui Tribal Literature*. Tucson: University of Arizona Press, 1980.

———, and Felipe S. Molina. *Yaqui Deer Songs / Maso Bwikam*. Tucson: University of Arizona Press, 1987.

Foster, George M. "The Current Status of Mexican Indian Folklore Studies," *JAF* 61 (1948): 368–82.

*———. *Sierra Popoluca Folklore and Beliefs.* University of California Publications in American Archaeology and Ethnology, vol. 42, no. 2. Berkeley, 1945. Cited as Foster 1945a.

†———. "Some Characteristics of Mexican Indian Folklore," *JAF* 58 (1945): 225–35. Cited as Foster 1945b.

Fought, John G. *Chorti (Mayan) Texts* 1. Philadelphia: University of Pennsylvania Press, 1972.

Furbee-Losee, Louanna, ed. *Mayan Texts.* 3 vols. Chicago: University of Chicago Press, 1976–80.

Furst, Jill Leslie. *Codex Vindobonensis Mexicanus I: A Commentary.* State University of New York at Albany, Institute for Mesoamerican Studies, 1978.

Furst, Peter T., and Salomón Nahmad. *Mitos y artes huicholes.* Mexico: Secretaría de Educación Pública, 1972.

Gamiz, Everardo. *Monografía de la nación tepehuana que habita en la region sur del estado de Durango.* Mexico: Gamiz, 1948.

Gibson, Lorna F., and Donald and Anne Olson. "Four Pame Texts," *Tlalocan,* 4 (1963): 125–43.

*Giddings, Ruth Warner. *Yaqui Myths and Legends.* Tucson: University of Arizona Press, 1959. Originally published as Anthropological Paper No. 2, University of Arizona, 1959.

Gifford, E. W., and R. H. Lowie. "Notes of the Akwa'ala Indians of Lower California," *University of California Publications in American Archaeology and Ethnology,* vol. 23, no. 7, pp. 339–52. Berkeley, 1928.

González Casanova, Pablo. *Cuentos indígenas.* 2d ed. Mexico: UNAM, 1965.

González Cruz, Genaro. "La historia de Tamakastsiin," *Estudios de Cultura Náhuatl* 17 (1984): 205–25.

Gordon, G. B. "Guatemala Myths," *Museum Journal* 6 (1915): 103–44. University of Pennsylvania.

†Gossen, Gary. *Chamulas in the World of the Sun: Time and Space in a Maya Oral Tradition.* Cambridge, Mass.: Harvard University Press, 1974.

———. "Two Creation Texts from Chamula, Chiapas," *Tlalocan* 8 (1980): 131–65.

Griffen, William B. *Notes on Seri Indian Culture, Sonora, Mexico.* Gainesville: University of Florida Press, 1959.

Grigsby, Thomas L. "In the Cosmic Warehouse: The Survival of a Cave Cult in Central Mexico." Typescript, n.d., in the possession of Thomas Grigsby, Dept. of Anthropology, Oregon State University, Corvallis.

Guiteras-Holmes, C[alixta]. *Perils of the Soul: The World View of a Tzotzil Indian.* New York: The Free Press of Glencoe / Crowell-Collier, 1961.

Hagen, V. Wolfgang von. *The Jicaque (Torrupan) Indians of Honduras.* Indian Notes and Monographs, no. 53. New York: Museum of the American Indian, 1943.

179

Hartman, C. V. "Mythology of the Aztecs of Salvador," *JAF* 20 (1907): 143–47.

Henson, Lance. *Another Song for America.* Norman, Okla.: Point Riders Press / Cottonwood Arts Foundation, 1987.

"Historias aportadas por las Hermanas de la Caridad de Santa Ana, Escuela de Amubre," *Tradición Oral Indígena Costarricense,* vol. 2, nos. 1–2, pp. 5–12. San José: Universidad de Costa Rica, Departamento de Antropología, 1984.

"Historias recogidas en Coroma, Coen y Amubre," *Tradición Oral Indígena Costarricense,* vol. 2, nos. 1–2, pp. 27–33. San José: Universidad de Costa Rica, Departamento de Antropología, 1984.

"Historias recopiladas en la comunidad de Dulurpe," *Tradición Oral Indígena Costarricense,* vol. 2, nos. 3–4, pp. 31–32. San José: Universidad de Costa Rica, Departamento de Antropología, 1987.

"History of the Mexicans as Told by Their Paintings" (ed. Henry Phillips, Jr.), *Proceedings of the American Philosophical Society* 21 (1883–84): 616–51. 1884.

"Histoyre du Mechique: manuscrit français inédit du XVIe siècle" (ed. Edouard de Jonghe), *Journal de la Société des Américanistes de Paris,* n.s., 2 (1905): 1–41.

Hobgood, John. "The Ixcaitiung or Ruling Man and the Chul: A Tepehuan Epic," *Proceedings of the* 38th International Congress of Americanists, pt. 2, pp. 401–11. Munich, 1970.

Holland, William R., and Roland G. Tharp. "Highland Maya Psychotherapy," *American Anthropologist,* n.s., 66 (1964): 41–52.

Hollenbach, Barbara K. "A Copala Trique Deluge Story," *Latin American Indian Literatures* 6 (1982): 114–25.

Hollenbach, Elena E. de. "El mundo animal en el folklore de los triques de Copala," *Tlalocan,* 8 (1980): 437–90.

———. "El origen del sol y de la luna: cuatro versiones en el trique de Copala," *Tlalocan,* 7 (1977): 123–70.

Hoogshagen, Searle. "La creación de sol y la luna según los mixes de Coatlán, Oaxaca," *Tlalocan,* 6 (1971): 337–46.

†Horcasitas, Fernando. "An Analysis of the Deluge Myth in Mesoamerica," *The Flood Myth* (ed. Alan Dundes), 183–219. Berkeley: University of California Press, 1988.

———. "La narrativa oral náhuatl," *Estudios de Cultura Náhuatl* 13 (1978): 177–209.

———, and Sarah O. de Ford. *Los cuentos en náhuatl de doña Luz Jiménez.* Mexico: UNAM, 1979.

Houwald, Götz von, and Francisco Rener. *Mayangna yulnina kulna balna / Tradiciones orales de los indios sumus / Múndliche Uberlieferungen der Sumu-Indianer.* Bonner Amerikanistische Studien 11. Bonn, West Germany: Seminar fúr Völkerkunde, Universität Bonn, 1984.

Incháustegui, Carlos. *Relatos del mundo mágico mazateco.* Mexico: INAH, 1977.

Irigoyen Rascón, Fructuoso. *Cerocahui: una comunidad en la Tarahumara.* Mexico: UNAM, 1974.

180

Ixtlilxóchitl, Fernando de Alva. *Obras históricas* (ed. Edmundo O'Gorman). 2 vols. Mexico: UNAM, 1975–77.

Joralemon, Peter David. *A Study of Olmec Iconography*. Washington, D.C.: Dumbarton Oaks, 1971.

Kannik, Preben. *The Flag Book*. New York: M. Barrows, 1959.

Kirchhoff, Paul. "Mesoamerica: Its Geographic Limits, Ethnic Composition and Cultural Characteristics," *Heritage of Conquest* (ed. Sol Tax), 17–30. Chicago: University of Chicago Press, 1952.

———, Lina Odena Gúemes, and Luis Reyes García, eds. *Historia tolteca-chichimeca*. Mexico: INAH, 1976.

Kroeber, A. L. *The Seri*. Southwest Museum Papers, no. 6. Los Angeles, 1931.

Kunst, J. "Some Animal Fables of the Chuh Indians," *JAF* 28 (1915): 353–57.

Kutscher, Gerdt, Gordon Brotherston, and Gúnter Vollmer. *Aesop in Mexico: A 16th-Century Aztec Version of Aesop's Fables*. Berlin: Gebr. Mann, 1987.

La Farge, Oliver. *Santa Eulalia: The Religion of a Cuchumatán Indian Town*. Chicago: University of Chicago Press, 1947.

———, and Douglas Byers. *The Year Bearer's People*. New Orleans: Department of Middle American Research, Tulane University, 1931.

Lasso de la Vega, Luis. *Huei tlamahuiçoltica . . .* (ed. Primo Feliciano Velázquez). Mexico: Carreño & Hijo, 1926.

Laughlin, Robert M. "In the Beginning: A Tale from the Mazatec," *Alcheringa*, no. 2 (1971): 37–52.

†*———. *Of Cabbages and Kings: Tales from Zinacantán*, Smithsonian Contributions to Anthropology, no. 25, 1977.

Lehmann, Walter. "Ergebnisse einer Forschungsreise in Mittelamerika und México 1907–1909," *Zeitschrift fúr Ethnologie* 42 (1910): 687–749.

———. "Ergebnisse einer mit Unterstützung der Notgemeinschaft der Deutschen Wissenschaft in den Jahren 1925/1926 ausgefúrten Forschungsreise nach Mexiko und Guatemala," *Anthropos* 23 (1928): 749–91.

———. *Zentral-Amerika*. 2 vols. Berlin: Dietrich Reimer, 1920.

Lemley, H. V. "Three Tlapaneco Stories from Tlacoapa, Guerrero," *Tlalocan* 3 (1949–57): 76–82.

Leslie, Charles, M. *Now We Are Civilized: A Study of the World View of the Zapotec Indians of Mitla, Oaxaca*. Detroit: Wayne State University Press, 1960.

López Avila, Carlos. Tlacotenco: tlahmachzaniltin ihuan tecuicame / Cuentos y canciones de mi pueblo. *Amerindia: revue d'ethnolinguistique amérindienne*, numéro spécial 5. Paris: Association d'Ethnolinguistique Amérindienne, 1984.

Lumholtz, Carl. *Unknown Mexico: Explorations in the Sierra Madre and Other Regions, 1890–1898*. 2 vols. New York: Dover, 1987.

McIntosh, John. "Cosmogonía huichol," *Tlalocan* 3 (1949–57): 14–21.

Madsen, William. *The Virgin's Children: Life in an Aztec Village Today*. Austin: University of Texas Press, 1960.

Mason, J. Alden. "Folk-Tales of the Tepecanos," *JAF* 27 (1914): 148–210.

Maurer Avalos, Eugenio, and Avelino Guzmán. "Una leyenda tseltal: el infierno o k'atimbak (calentar con huesos)," *Tlalocan*, 10 (1985): 257–72.

Mayers, Marvin. *Pokomchi Texts*. Norman: Summer Institute of Linguistics of the University of Oklahoma, 1958.

Mediz Bolio, Antonio. *The Land of the Pheasant and the Deer* (trans. Enid E. Perkins). Mérida, Yucatán: Dante, 1983.

Mendieta, Gerónimo de. *Historia eclesiástica indiana*. Mexico: Porrúa, 1971.

Mengin, Ernst. "Unos annales [sic] históricos de la nación mexicana: Die Manuscrits mexicains nr. 22 und 22 bis der Bibliothèque Nationale de Paris" [i.e., Anales de Tlatelolco], *Baessler-Archiv*, vol. 22, nos. 2–3. Berlin, 1939.

Merrifield, William R. "When the Sun Rose for the First Time: A Chinantec Creation Myth," *Tlalocan*, 5 (1967): 193–97.

Merrill, William L. *Rarámuri Souls*. Washington, D.C.: Smithsonian, 1988.

———. "Tarahumara Social Organization, Political Organization, and Religion," *Handbook of North American Indians*, vol. 10: Southwest (ed. Alfonso Ortiz), pp. 290–305. Washington, D.C.: Smithsonian, 1983.

Miles, Suzanne W. "Mam Residence and the Maize Myth," *Culture and History: Essays in Honor of Paul Radin* (ed. Stanley Diamond), pp. 430–36. New York: Columbia University Press, 1960.

Miller, Walter S. *Cuentos mixes*. Mexico: Instituto Nacional Indigenista, 1956.

Mixco, Mauricio J. *Kiliwa Texts: "When I Have Donned My Crest of Stars."* Anthropological Papers, no. 107. University of Utah, Salt Lake City, 1983.

———. "Textos para la etnohistoria en la frontera dominicana de Baja California," *Tlalocan*, 7 (1977): 205–26.

Montejo, Victor Dionicio. *El Kanil, Man of Lightning: A Legend of Jacaltenango, Guatemala*. Carrboro, N.C.: Signal Books, 1985.

———. "The Origin of Corn." Typescript, n.d.

Morales, Pablo. "Cuentos mames" (trans. Norman A. McQuown), Microfilm Collection of Manuscripts on Cultural Anthropology, no. 130. Joseph Regenstein Library, University of Chicago. 1977.

Morales Stewart, Rito. "Historias recopiladas en la comunidad de Katsi," *Tradición Oral Indígena Costarricense*, vol. 2, nos. 3–4, pp. 18–24. San José: Universidad de Costa Rica, Departamento de Antropología, 1987.

†Moreno de los Arcos, Roberto. "Los cinco soles cosmogónicos," *Estudios de Cultura Náhuatl* 7 (1967): 183–210.

Myerhoff, Barbara. *Peyote Hunt: The Sacred Journey of the Huichol Indians*. Ithaca, N.Y.: Cornell University Press, 1974.

Nash, June. *In the Eyes of the Ancestors: Belief and Behavior in a Maya Community*. New Haven: Yale University Press, 1970.

†Nicholson, Henry B. "Religion in Pre-Hispanic Mexico," *Handbook of Middle American Indians*, vol. 10 (Gordon F. Ekholm and Ignacio Bernal, eds.), pp. 395–446. Austin: University of Texas Press, 1971.

Nuttall, Zelia, ed. *The Book of the Life of the Ancient Mexicans* [Codex Magliabechiano]. Berkeley: University of California Press, 1903.

———. *The Codex Nuttall*. With a new introductory text by Arthur G. Miller.

New York: Dover, 1975.

Oakes, Maud. *The Two Crosses of Todos Santos: Survivals of Mayan Religious Ritual.* New York: Bollingen / Pantheon, 1951.

Ochurte, Rufino, and Mauricio J. Mixco. "The God-Child's Vengeance: A Kiliwa Story from Baja California," *Alcheringa*, n.s., 3 (1977): 55–62.

Orellana, Sandra L. "Folk Literature of the Tzutujil Maya," *Anthropos* 70 (1975): 839–76.

Oviedo [y Valdés], Gonzalo Fernández de. *Historia general y natural de las Indias.* 5 vols. Biblioteca de Autores Españoles, vols. 117–21. Madrid: Atlas, 1959.

Paredes, Américo. *Folktales of Mexico.* Chicago: University of Chicago Press, 1970.

Parsons, Elsie Clews. *Mitla, Town of the Souls: And Other Zapoteco-speaking Pueblos of Oaxaca, Mexico.* Chicago: University of Chicago Press, 1936.

Paz, Octavio. "Mexico and the United States" (trans. Rachel Phillips), *The New Yorker*, Sept. 17, 1979, pp. 136–53.

Pereira, Francisco. "Narraciones de Francisco Pereira," *Tradición Oral Indígena Costarricense*, vol. 1, no. 3, pp. 11–48. San José: Universidad de Costa Rica, Departamento de Antropología, 1983.

Petrich, Perla. "Los mochós cuentan de dónde vino el fuego," *Estudios de Cultura Maya* 16 (1985): 271–94.

Pineda, Vicente. *Historia de las sublevaciones indígenas habidas en el estado de Chiapas.* Chiapas: Tipografía del Gobierno, 1888.

Pittier de Fábrega, Henri. "Folk-Lore of the Bribri and Brunka Indians in Costa Rica," *JAF* 16 (1903): 1–9.

Portal, María Ana. *Cuentos y mitos en una zona mazateca.* Serie Antropología Social. Mexico: INAH, 1986.

Preuss, Konrad T. "Au sujet et caractère des mythes et des chants huichols que j'ai recueillis," *Revista del Instituto de Etnología de la Universidad Nacional de Tucuman*, vol. 2 (1932): 445–57. Tucuman, Argentina.

———. "Die Hochzeit des Maises und andere Geschichten der Huichol-Indianer," *Globus*, vol. 91, no. 12, pp. 185–92. Braunschweig, 1907.

*———. *Die Nayarit-Expedition*, vol. 1: Die Religion der Cora-Indianer. Leipzig: B. G. Teubner, 1912.

Recinos, Adrián, Delia Goetz, and D. J. Chonay, eds. *The Annals of the Cakchiquels [and] Title of the Lords of Totonicapán.* Norman: University of Oklahoma Press, 1953.

Recinos, Adrián, Delia Goetz, and Sylvanus G. Morley. *Popol Vuh: The Sacred Book of the Ancient Quiché Maya.* Norman: University of Oklahoma Press, 1950.

Redfield, Margaret Park. "The Folk Literature of a Yucatecan Town," *Contributions to American Archaeology*, no. 13, Carnegie Institution of Washington, 1935.

Redfield, Robert. "Notes on San Antonio Palopo." Microfilm Collection of Manuscripts on Cultural Anthropology, no. 4. Joseph Regenstein Library, University of Chicago. 1945.

———, and Alfonso Villa R[ojas]. *Chan Kom: A Maya Village*. Washington: Carnegie Institution of Washington, 1934.

Reina, Ruben E. *The Law of the Saints: A Pokomam Pueblo and Its Community Culture*. Indianapolis: Bobbs-Merrill, 1966.

Reyes García, Luis, and Dieter Christensen. *Der Ring aus Tlalocan / El anillo de Tlalocan*. Berlin: Gebr. Mann, 1976.

Riley, Carroll L., and John Hobgood. "A Recent Nativistic Movement among the Southern Tepehuan Indians," *Southwestern Journal of Anthropology* 15 (1959): 355–60.

Rodríguez Prampolini, Ida, ed. *A través de la frontera*. Mexico: Centro de Estudios Económicos y Sociales del Tercer Mundo / Instituto de Investigaciones Estéticas, UNAM, 1983.

Roys, Ralph. *The Book of Chilam Balam of Chumayel*. Norman: University of Oklahoma Press, 1967.

Sahagún, Bernardino de. *Códice florentino*. 3 vols. Mexico: Secretaría de Gobernación, 1979.

———. *Florentine Codex: General History of the Things of New Spain* (ed. Arthur J. O. Anderson and Charles E. Dibble). Parts 1–13 (introductory volume and books 1–12). 1st ed. Santa Fe, N. Mex.: School of American Research and University of Utah Press, 1950–82.

———. *Historia general de las cosas de Nueva España* (ed. Angel M. Garibay K.). 4 vols. 2d ed. Mexico: Porrúa, 1969.

Sandstrom, Alan R., ed. "Myths recounted by Jesus Bautista Hernandez... Puyecaco, Ixhuatlán de Madero, Veracruz... January 1986." Transcribed by Daniele Bafile and trans. from the Nahuatl by Guemes J. Typescript, n.d., in the possession of Alan Sandstrom, Dept. of Anthropology, Indiana University-Purdue University, Fort Wayne.

Sandstrom, Alan R., and Pamela E. Sandstrom. *Traditional Papermaking and Paper Cult Figures of Mexico*. Norman: University of Oklahoma Press, 1986.

Savala, Refugio. *The Autobiography of a Yaqui Poet* (ed. Kathleen M. Sands). Tucson: University of Arizona Press, 1980.

Scheffler, Lilian. *Cuentos y leyendas de México*. Mexico: Panorama, 1985.

Schele, Linda, and Mary Ellen Miller. *The Blood of Kings: Dynasty and Ritual in Maya Art*. New York and Fort Worth: George Braziller / Kimbell Art Museum, 1986.

Schoembs, Jakob. *Material zur Sprache von Comalapa in Guatemala*. Dortmund: F. W. Ruhfus, 1905.

Schultze Jena, Leonhard. *Indiana*, vol. 2: Mythen in der Muttersprache der Pipil von Izalco in El Salvador. Jena, Germany: Gustav Fischer, 1935.

Séjourné, Laurette. "Los otomies de Mezquital," *Cuadernos Americanos* 66 (1952): 17–34.

Septimo, Roger, and Luz Graciela Joly. *Kugue kira nie ngabere / Sucesos antiguos dichos en guaymí*. David, Panama: Asociación Panameña de Antropología, 1986.

[Serrano y Sanz, Manuel.] *Relaciones históricas y geográficas de América Central.*

Colección de libros y documentos referentes a la historia de América, vol. 8. Madrid: Librería General de Victoriano Suárez, 1908.

*Shaw, Mary, ed. *According to Our Ancestors: Folk Texts from Guatemala and Honduras.* Norman: Summer Institute of Linguistics of the University of Oklahoma, 1971.

Siegel, Morris. "The Creation Myth and Acculturation in Acatán, Guatemala," JAF 56 (1943): 120–26.

Skinner, Alanson. "Notes on the Bribri of Costa Rica," *Indian Notes and Monographs* 4 (1920): 37–106.

Slocum, Marianna C. "The Origin of Corn and Other Tzeltal Myths," *Tlalocan*, 5 (1965): 1–45.

Spicer, Edward H. *Pascua: A Yaqui Village in Arizona.* Chicago: University of Chicago Press, 1940.

———. *Potam: A Yaqui Village in Sonora.* Memoirs, vol. 56, no. 4, pt. 2. American Anthropological Association, 1954.

———. *The Yaquis: A Cultural History.* Tucson: University of Arizona Press, 1980.

Stephens, John L. *Incidents of Travel in Central America, Chiapas and Yucatan.* 2 vols. New York: Dover, 1969.

Steward, Julian H. *Handbook of South American Indians,* vol. 4: The Circum-Caribbean Tribes. Bureau of American Ethnology, Bulletin 143, vol. 4. 1948.

Stiles, Neville. "The Creation of the Coxtecame, The Discovery of Corn, The Rabbit and the Moon and Other Nahuatl Folk Narratives," *Latin American Indian Literatures Journal* 1 (1985): 97–121. Cited as Stiles 1985a.

———. "El diluvio y otros relatos nahuas de la Huasteca hidalguense," *Tlalocan*, 10 (1985): 15–32. Cited as Stiles 1985b.

———. "The Man, the Stag and the Transforming Women: The Nahua View of Animal Survival," *Latin American Indian Literatures* 8 (1984): 84–91.

Stoll, David. *Fishers of Men or Founders of Empire? The Wycliffe Bible Translators in Latin America.* London: Zed Press, 1983.

*Stone, Doris. *The Talamancan Tribes of Costa Rica.* Papers of the Peabody Museum of Archaeology and Ethnology, Harvard University, vol. 43, no. 2. Cambridge, Mass., 1962.

Straatman, Silke. *Die Wollbilder der Huichol-Indianer: Eine Indianerstamm stellt seine Mythen dar.* Marburger Studien zun Völkerkunde, 6. Marburg: Völkerkundliches Seminar der Phillipps-Universität, 1988.

Stubblefield, Morris, and Carol Stubblefield. "The Story of Lay and Gisaj: A Zapotec Sun and Moon Myth," *Tlalocan*, 6 (1969): 46–62.

*Taggart, James M. *Nahuatl Myth and Social Structure.* Austin: University of Texas Press, 1983.

Taracena, Berta. *Diego Rivera: su obra mural en la ciudad de México.* Mexico: Galería de Arte Misrachi, 1981.

Tax, Sol. "Folk Tales in Chichicastenango: An Unsolved Puzzle," JAF 62 (1949): 125–35.

185

———. "Panajachel: Field Notes." Microfilm Collection of Manuscripts on Cultural Anthropology, no. 29. Joseph Regenstein Library, University of Chicago. 1950.

Tedlock, Dennis. *The Spoken Word and the Work of Interpretation*. Philadelphia: University of Pennsylvania Press, 1983.

———, trans. *Popol Vuh: The Mayan Book of the Dawn of Life*. New York: Simon & Schuster, 1985.

Thompson, J. E. S. *Ethnology of the Mayas of Southern and Central British Honduras*. Anthropological Series, vol. 17, no. 2. Chicago: Field Museum of Natural History, 1930.

———. *Maya History and Religion*. Norman: University of Oklahoma Press, 1970.

Toor, Frances. *A Treasury of Mexican Folkways*. New York: Crown, 1947.

Tozzer, Alfred M. *A Comparative Study of the Mayas and the Lacandones*. New York: Macmillan, 1907.

———, ed. *Landa's Relación de las Cosas de Yucatan*. New York: Kraus Reprint, 1966.

Valentini, Philipp J. J. "Trique Theogony: An Alleged Specimen of Ancient Mexican Folk-lore," JAF 12 (1899): 38–42.

Vázquez, Juan Adolfo. Review of Marie-Noëlle Chamoux, "Orphée nahua," *Amerindia* 5 (1980): 113–22. In *Latin American Indian Literatures* 6 (1982): 148–49. Review of Rodrigo Salazar, *Las leyendas del Duchi*. In *Latin American Indian Literatures* 3 (1979): 93–95.

Velázquez, Primo Feliciano. *Códice Chimalpopoca: Anales de Cuauhtitlan y Leyenda de los soles*. Mexico: UNAM, 1945.

Villa R[ojas], Alfonso. *The Maya of East Central Quintana Roo*. Washington, D.C.: Carnegie Institution of Washington, 1945.

———, J. M. Velasco Toro, F. Baez-Jorge, F. Córdoba, and N. D. Thomas. *Los zoques de Chiapas*. Mexico: Instituto Nacional Indigenista, 1975.

Villanueva, Clementino, and Carmen Cubero Venegas. "Kotzobawa," *Tradición Oral Indígena Costarricense*, vol. 1, no. 3, p. 5. San José: Universidad de Costa Rica, Departamento de Antropología, [1983].

Wauchope, Robert, ed. *Handbook of Middle American Indians*. 16 vols. Austin: University of Texas Press, 1964–76.

*Weitlaner, Roberto. *Relatos, mitos y leyendas de la Chinantla* (ed. María Sara Molinari et al.) Mexico: Instituto Nacional Indigenista, 1977.

———, and Gabriel de Cicco. "La jerarquía de los dioses zapotecos de sur," *Proceedings of the* 34th *International Congress of Americanists*, pp. 695–710. 1962.

Williams García, Roberto. *Mitos tepehuas*. Mexico: Secretaría de Educación Pública, 1972.

Young, Philip D. *Ngawbe: Tradition and Change among the Western Guaymí of Panama*. Urbana: University of Illinois Press, 1971.

*Ziehm, Elsa, ed. *Nahua-Texte aus San Pedro Jícora in Durango*. Aufgezeichnet von Konrad Theodor Preuss. 3 vols. Berlin: Gebr. Mann, 1968–76.

Zingg, Robert M. "The Genuine and Spurious Values in Tarahumara Culture,"

American Anthropologist n.s., 44 (1942): 78–92.

———. The Huichols: Primitive Artists. Milwood, N.Y.: Kraus Reprint, 1977.